SOME OF MY BEST JOKES ARE JEWISH!

by *Gerry Blumenfeld*

with sketches by *Bob Anthony*

CONTENTS

Dedicated to my husband, Harold, who has been my captive and most appreciative audience through the years.

PREFACE

The Jewish people wandered through many lands and suffered many hardships. Sometimes the only precious possession they carried with them was a sense of humor.

They told stories—some with a philosophical saltiness; some subtle; some reached a ridiculous height, or a pathetic low. But they laughed. Perhaps this ability to laugh, mainly at themselves, helped them to endure.

In this book, I have compiled my favorite Yiddish stories...some old, some new, some orginal and some even true.

HAVE A LAUGH!

Gerry Blumenfeld

CULTURE—
"SHMULTURE"

While walking to his office on Seventh Avenue, a man was startled by a slap on the back and a loud voice that shrieked, "Well, if it ain't mine old pal, Izzy Epstein! How's by you?"

"Shhhh!'" replied his old friend, "I'm no longer Epstein. I changed my name to Eldridge."

"So where did you get the name 'Eldridge', Izzy?"

Again he was shushed and his friend said, "What do you mean 'where'? Don't you remember, twenty years ago we both lived on Eldridge Street? Well, that's where I got the name. And by the way, I'm no more 'Izzy'. I'm now known by two initials...C. R.!"

"So where did you get the initials C. R?"

"What do you mean 'where'? Don't you remember we lived on Eldridge, corner Rivington?"

Two Yiddish poets had been bitter rivals for years. Somehow their paths had not crossed for sometime. One evening, they met in the Russian Tea Room.

As they ate, they talked. Each tried to impress the other with fancy boasts about how his career had flourished.

The first poet, Joseph Koenig said, "Yes, since we last met, you have no idea how popular my poetry has become. Yes, my good friend...my readers have doubled!"

"Mazel tov!" said the second poet, Yakov Gastner, "I had no idea you got married!"

A Jewish family moved into a swanky, uncontrolled and overpriced apartment on Sutton Place in Manhattan.

The first thing they did, after setting the furniture in place, was to put a "mezuzah" on the door.

A letter arrived from the management asking them to remove it. They were advised that the house was equipped not only with Master TV antennas, but with master "mezuzahs" as well.

It was a balmy summer day at Grossinger's in the Catskills. The free dancing lesson for guests was held out on the large terrace and had just ended.

One of the guests, still panting from the lesson, walked over to another guest who was sitting on the side-lines reading his New York Times.

"Hi! Max!" said the dancing guest.

The studious one looked up from his paper and answered, "Hi!...by the way, what do you think of Katanga?"

"Please! I'm having troubles enough with the twist!"

Three partners owned a small movie chain on the lower East Side. They were eager to expand. They learned of a run-down movie house that was for sale in the swank Sutton Area of New York and purchased it, with a view to making it a fine art movie.

The renovation began and was progressing well. They had all the fixtures painted white, the walls red with red carpeting laid wall to wall. It was beginning to take on an air of elegance. They now had to make a decision about the seats.

"I think leather seats would be best," said Louis. "In case any of the customers put chewing gum on them, it's easier to remove gum from leather."

"What kind of talk is this about chewing gum?" raged Benny. "Did you forget this is gonna be a high-tone movie house with fancy-shmancy customers...excuse me, patrons! I think the seats should be plush...because plush is lush!"

The argument continued.

"Well, let's ask Max. He's a partner too! Max, what do you think the seats should be covered with?" inquired Louis.

"If you want my opinion, I'll tell you. As far as I'm concerned, I'm interested in only one thing...that they should be covered with backsides!"

The Horowitz family moved from the Bronx to Woodmere and joined the country club. Mr. Horowitz was gregarious and likeable and they began to receive invitations to the homes of the various members of the club. After each of these dinner parties, the Horowitzs quarreled.

He raged, "At home, you ya-ta-ta-ta without a stop. As soon as we get among people, you shut up like a clam! I warn you...if you sit there like a dumbbell again without opening your mouth, I'm going to be furious!"

The following week, they were invited to another dinner party at the sumptuous home of the Waldman's. The dinner was superb; the conversation scintillating. Mr. Horowitz, as usual, was garrulous. He even told a couple of amusing stories. His wife ate in silence, looking miserable as her husband shot menacing glances in her direction. But still not a word from Mrs. Horowitz.

The waitress brought a large silver tray on which was a magnificent silver coffee set.

Mrs. Waldman said, "Daphne, you may pour the coffee in here for the men. We ladies will have ours in the library."

At last...Mrs. Horowitz opened her mouth and in a surprised tone said, "My, my! I didn't know the library was open on Sundays!"

Mrs. Goldspritzer contacted Woods and Woods, Interior Decorators to the trade and asked them to send one of their best consultants to her home. The appointment was made and a meticulously dressed young man called on her.

She explained she would like her whole house redecorated and that she had in the neighborhood of $25,000 to spend.

The decorator asked what period she preferred and she said she didn't know. He said, "Would you like a contemporary home?"

"No!"

"Italian provincial?"

"No!"

After mentioning seven or eight periods and getting a "no" answer to each, he said, "Madam, if you wish Woods and Woods to work with you, you're just going to have to give me some idea as to period."

"Look, my dear young man," she said. "I want you shull fix me up a house, it should be so gudgeous that when my friends walk in, they should take one look... and drop dead! Period!"

A fire broke out in a hotel in the Catskills. To alert the guests, a voice sounded the alarm by yelling, "Fire! Fire! Cha-cha-cha! Fire! Fire! Cha-cha-cha!"

The Goldfishers had a brilliant son, Saul, whose main interest in life was science. He graduated from City College magna cum laude and was awarded fellowships for graduate work at Harvard, M.I.T. and Princeton. This was a difficult decision to make but he chose M.I.T.

He received his master's degree as well as many other awards for scholastic achievement. His parents glowed with pride.

Mr. Goldfisher said, "Son, we want to get you a nice graduation present. We'd like to be able to get you a car or a boat or something like that but you know we can't afford it. But how about a nice record player or a nice watch, anything you want, we'll get you!"

"Gosh, Dad, I do appreciate your generosity but there's only one thing I'd like above all else. I'd be very happy if you bought me a pair of Guinea pigs!"

Papa was dumbfounded! He quickly recovered.

"Son! That's out of the question! You know, in the first place, that mama keeps a kosher house! In the second place, I'm convinced that better you should have gone to Harvard! I'm sure that there, at least, they'd have taught you that the word is 'Italian'!"

A Texan flashed the operator at the Waldorf and asked to be connected with the box office at Carnegie Hall.

A man's voice answered and the Texan said, "Ah would like four of your best tickets for tonight's concert. Ah want to hear mah feller-Texan, Van Cliburn play."

The voice answered that they were completely sold out. The Texan persisted that he'd pay any amount, that he simply had to be at the concert.

"Sorry, sir, there isn't a ticket to be had. Even all the standing room is gone."

"Wah, that's ridiculous!" bellowed the Texan. "Ah'll come over there and buy Carnegie Hall, if need be, but ah'll heah this feller, Van, play!"

He rushed down into the street, hailed a cab and said to the driver, who happened to be Jewish:

"Do you-all know the best way to get to Carnegie Hall?"

"Practice, my boy, practice!"

Mr. Fafoofnick moved to a restricted community in the suburbs, changed his religion and changed his name to Field.

With his new environment, he decided to divest himself of all stigma of his former religion.

After his belongings were unpacked, he 'phoned the art gallery where he had purchased his works of art. He asked the art dealer to please pick up his Epstein and substitute it for a Goya.*

---

*Goya in Yiddish is a non-Jewish woman.

Roz Komackowitz moved to Kings Point and was invited to join a canasta group. She complained bitterly to her husband that she had had a miserable time even though she had enjoyed the game itself.

"So, what are you miserable about? Didn't you like your new friends?"

"No! They seem very nice but I was never so humiliated in my whole life! When we sat down to have coffee, all the girls were talking about their trips to Europe, to Israel, around the world! They'll think I'm a regular dope with nothing to talk about! Where did you ever take me? To Coney Island!"

"So, tell them you've already been around the world and you have no place else to go now!"

"Please...Ernie, stop making like Milton Berle. I'm serious!"

"All right, Roz, I have a solution. I'll bring you some travel folders, you'll look them over and then you can make believe you traveled too!"

The following week, Roz went to the canasta game again. As they sipped their coffee, one of the girls started to talk about her recent trip to Europe.

Roz said, "My husband and I went to Europe last summer too! We had a fabulous time! We were even invited to the palace at Monaco to have cocktails with Prince Rainier and Grace Kelly!"

One of the girls gushed, "Oh, how exciting! Tell us about it! What were they like?"

"Well, he's a regular Prince Charming just like in the fairy tales! And her...do I have to tell you? She's a living doll!"

One of the other girls asked, "Did you go to Rome too?"

"Naturally!" said Roz. "And what's more we had a private audience with the Pope!"

"A *private* audience?" asked another player, very much impressed. "Why, that's terrific! What is the new Pope like?"

"Oh!" declared Roz. "He is absolutely marvelous! His wife I could live without"

Emma and Pincus Teitlebaum joined a beach club at Atlantic Beach. They didn't know anyone at the club and the first few weeks, sat off by themselves near the pool.

Emma became acquainted with a woman in the next cabana and she invited the Teitlebaums to sit with their group. On Sunday, Pincus went along and he too joined them.

As they sat around the pool, the conversation took an interesting turn. Someone mentioned how sad it was that two of our great writers, Hemingway and Faulkner, had recently passed on. Someone else spoke about Sandburg, Frost and T. S. Eliot, Pincus occasionally joined in the conversation but Emma sat silent throughout.

On the way home, Pincus began to yell at his wife. "For God's Sake! Can't you open your mouth once in awhile! You sit there like the cat got not only your tongue but your brains too!"

Emma sulked and said nothing. She was determined though, that next week, she would make a contribution to the conversation.

The following Sunday, again they were all gathered around the pool. One of the women was ecstatic! She had been to the new Philharmonic Hall at Lincoln Center and heard an all-Tchaikovsky concert! "I just adore his Nutcracker Suite!"

Turning to Emma, she said, "Are you at all familiar with Tchaikovsky?"

"Familiar?" answered Emma. "Why, last week when our car was laid up, I took the number four bus to the beach. And who should be sitting next to me but him! He was very friendly and he talked to me all the way until he got off the bus!"

There was dead silence! Happily, someone suggested going into the pool.

Pincus was furious! On the way home in the car, he sat frozen without saying a word. Emma could see something was wrong.

"All right, Pincus, come out with it! I can see you're mad at me. What did I say that was wrong?"

Pincus roared, "What did you say that was wrong? How stupid can you be? How many times do I have to tell you...the number four bus doesn't go to the beach!"

On her very first trip to Paris, Mrs. Gingold quickly changed her clothes and rushed out to do some shopping. She dashed to the Maison de Blanc and as she entered, a vendeuse welcomed her.

"Bon jour, madame."

Mrs. Gingold answered, "Bon jour," and rushed over to a table where they displayed beautiful tablecloths.

She inspected them all, picked out the most gorgeous of the lot, looked for the price-tag but found it was written in code. She turned to the vendeuse and in her very best French asked, "Madame, combien coute cette...tishtach?"

"Madame, cette tishtach coute mille franc."

"Mille franc pour cette...shmattah!" inquired Mrs. Gingold.

"Madame, cette tishtach n'est pas un shmattah; c'est une grande...metziah!"

Mrs. Gingold angrily retorted, "J'ai dit une shmattah et une shmattah!" and she walked out of the shop!

The weary vendeuse turned to another vendeuse, shaking her head disgustedly and commented, "Les Americains!...quelle chutzpah!"

Mr. and Mrs. Pearlman had not had the benefit of formal education but they decided their daughter, Naomi, would get the best they could afford.

After graduation from college, the Pearlmans sent Naomi off to Paris to study at the Sorbonne. When she returned, she met a nice young lawyer and they were married. About a year later, Naomi announced she was expecting a baby. Her parents were besides themselves with joy. This was to be their first grandchild and mama hovered over her daughter nervously.

When Naomi was rushed to the hospital, mama accompanied her and would not leave her for a moment. The obstetrician suggested that, perhaps, Mrs. Pearlman might wait outside but she would have no part of it.

"Naomi kept on moaning, "Mon Dieu! Mon Dieu!"*

Mama pleaded with the doctor. "Do something! She's ready to give birth!"

"Not yet," assured the doctor.

Naomi kept moaning, "Mon Dieu!" and mama begged the doctor to do something. The doctor, annoyed by the mother's insistence, again repeated, "I assure you, she's not ready yet."

A few minutes later, Naomi shrieked, "Oy gevalt,* mama, get the doctor!"

The doctor rushed into the room and said, "Please leave, Mrs. Pearlman, your daughter is now ready for the delivery room!"

Mon Dieu—"My God"—in French*
*gevalt—*help—Yiddish*

In the old Czarist days in a small town in Russia, word began to spread that something new had come to Moscow...something known as the "theatre."

The elders in the town decided to send a representative to observe this phenomenon and report back. If it was as remarkable as they had heard, perhaps, they too could set one up in their town as well.

And so a carriage and horses with Sholom and his driver, Ivan, left for Moscow. Many weeks passed, for it was a long journey. Finally Sholom returned. The townspeople gathered at the town meeting place to hear the report.

Sholom rose and said, "My friends, I am sorry to have to report to you that the whole thing was nothing with nothing. In a big room with many seats, there was a large platform. Out on the platform, came a young man and a young girl. When he wanted, she didn't want; when she wanted, he didn't want. And when they both wanted already, somebody dropped down a big white sheet in front of them!"

EVERYONE'S
A PHILOSOPHER

Way back in the days when the Czars ruled in Russia, Avram boarded a train for the first time in his life. He sat back in his seat, prepared to gaze out the window and enjoy the rolling countryside. A man came in and sat opposite him. After a moment of silence, Avram was greeted with a big "Shalom, Avram! Do you remember me? My name is Muttel. How is your health?"

Avram answered, "My health? Ehhhh!" nodding his head as he spoke.

There was a long pause. Muttel broke the silence.

"So where are you going, Avram?"

"Ehhhhh...I'm taking a little ride to Minsk."

Muttel went into a strange interlude. He began to reason to himself: Avram tells me he's taking a little ride to Minsk. If he was going to Minsk, would he tell me, practically a perfect stranger? No! So if he's not going to Minsk, where could he be going? One place. Pinsk!

So what is he going to do in Pinsk? Only one thing. After all, a bachelor he still is, so he's going to Pinsk to get married. So whom could he be marrying in Pinsk? In Pinsk, there are only three Jewish families he could possibly know...the Pitzicks, the Rabinowitzs and the Pupkowitzs.

To the Pitzicks, he wouldn't be going. Pitzick has only sons. The Rabinowitzs have two daughters but they're both married. But the Pupkowitzs, ah! They have three daughters...Sonia, Tanya and Luba. Sonia is too young; Tanya, well, not so good looking; ah! but Luba, a living doll! So, one thing...he's going to marry Luba Pupkowitz.

Muttel called across to Avram, "Avram, my friend, allow me to congratulate you on your forthcoming marriage to Luba Pupkowitz!"

Avram, startled, stammered, "Well, well...how do you know that?"

"How do I know that?" replied Muttel. "Why, you practically told me!"

Hard times had befallen Mendel Shmendrick. He had lost his business and had to beg for money for food.

He stopped a man on the street and asked him for three cents for a cup of coffee.

"Where can you get a cup of coffee for three cents?" the man asked. "What do you mean 'where'? who buys retail?"

On the corner of Broadway and Canal Street, Izzy ran into Jake.

"Oy! It's good to see you, Jake, So how are you?"

With a shrug and a grunt, he answered "Ehhhhh...!"

"And how's your wife?"

"Eh-eh!"

"And how is business?"

"Mm-mmm!"

"Well, goodbye, Jake. It was nice to see you. And believe me, there's nothing like a good heart-to-heart talk with a friend!"

Two patriarchal elderly Jews sat drinking glass of tea after glass of tea without a word being exchanged between them. After about two hours of silence, one sighed a deep, deep sigh and said, "Oy vay!" His friend answered, "You're telling me!"

When the United Nations directive forced the English, French and Israelis to withdraw from their Suez adventure, one Israeli remarked sadly to another:

"It's a shame! If they had let us go on for just one more day, the Suez would have been ours!"

"Don't feel so bad," consoled his friend. "Who needs it? No boardwalk!"

A few days after the new Pope had been elected, Cardinal Sicola had dinner with an old friend, Rabbi Parreira.

They chatted about many things and the Rabbi noticed that his friend seemed rather dejected.

"Dear friend," said the Rabbi. "You seem disturbed. Is it anything that you would care to discuss with me?"

"Well, Rabbi, it's simply this. You know, of course, that I did not labor under any illusion that I might be elected. I just never dreamed though that I was so unpopular not to have received even one vote!"

"My dear Cardinal," consoled the Rabbi. "Dismiss any such thought from your mind immediately. You are indeed beloved and held in very high esteem by your colleagues. I know what must have been on their minds. Each one undoubtedly figured if he voted for you and you were elected, how would it sound to call you Pope-Sicola!"

15

The world had gone to pot, as far as Yankel was concerned. Business was so bad, he couldn't meet his bills. He was telling his troubles to his oldest friend.

"Yankel, no matter how bad things are, it could be worse!"

Yankel was exasperated.

"My friend, you drive me crazy with your cheerful epigrams!"

"But it's true, Yankel, when a person's in trouble, if he searches his soul, he'll always find something to be thankful for."

"And what have I got to be thankful for?"

"Be thankful you're not one of your creditors!"

Two old cronies sat on the sand in Miami Beach, making appropriate comments, as they watched the young girls pass by.

After a pause in their conversation, Jake said, "Tell me, Abe, are you still interested in making love?"

After contemplating the question for several seconds, he answered, "Ehhhhh!"

"How often?" asked his friend. "Every week?"

"No."

"Every month?"

"No."

"So, how often?"

"Once a winter," came the retort.

"Jake," the inquisitor went on. "Have you made love yet this winter?"

Abe raised both arms, looked around, taking in the whole scene...the blue sky, the white fleecy clouds, the calm ocean, the hot sand and said petulantly, "This... you call a winter?"

In a poor town in pre-war Poland, there lived a wise and kindly old rabbi. He was revered by his congregation but, unfortunately, they could not pay him well. He rode around comforting the sick on a horse. He loved the animal and cared for him with tender, loving care.

One day while making his rounds, one of his parishioners asked, "Rabbi, how come your horse's coat always looks so much better than yours?"

"There's a simple answer, my son," answered the rabbi. "You see, I take care of my horse; my congregation takes care of me!"

A venerable old Jewish gentleman was day-dreaming while sunning himself on a bench on the boardwalk at Atlantic City.

His reverie was disturbed when another man approached and asked, "Can I join you?"

"What's the matter, maybe I'm coming apart?"

Among the Hassidim in Williamsburg in Brooklyn, little synagogues spring up in stores, empty lofts, in any available place that will accommodate ten ultra-orthodox Jews. The place of worship is sometimes referred to as the "shteebel." The members usually spend more hours in the "shteebel" than in their own homes. It is a place for worship; for arguing politics; a haven from a nagging wife, or for a lonesome man without a wife.

In one of these "shteebels," Chaim Shmiel made an announcement to his colleagues. His son had a very good season and as a gift to him, had arranged for him to visit his family in the old country. His friends took out the bottle of sacramental wine, toasted his good health and wished him a fine trip. He assured them he would return before the High Holidays to celebrate with them.

After Chaim Shmiel had gone, the members looked about them and realized their little "shteebel" was in a state of disrepair. The paint was peeling from the walls; the entire place was a mess! Some borrowed from their children and the work was begun.

The place was painted; chairs were repaired; and four shiny, brass cuspidors were bought on Allen Street as part of Operation Clean-Up. At last, everything was in readiness for the Holidays and as a homecoming surprise for Chaim Shmiel.

As soon as he returned, Chaim Shmiel ran to the "shteebel" for his morning prayers. The prayers over, he started to give his friends regards from their old cronies in Europe.

He put some snuff in his mouth and chewed on it as he talked. As he had always done, he started to clear his throat to expectorate on the floor.

Zacharia screamed, "Please, Chaim Shmiel, don't spit on the floor! Can't you see we fixed up the place?"

Pointing to the shiny new cuspidors, he continued, "Now, if you wanna spit, spit only in the spitoons!"

Chaim Shmiel grabbed his head in his two hands and with consternation in his voice, cried out, "Oy! Gevalt! What did you make here...a reform temple?"

A young man walked into a subway train, sat down and started reading his morning paper. He looked up and opposite him, beneath a "NO SMOKING" sign, sat an elderly Jewish gentleman smoking a cigar.

The young man assumed that the old man could not read English and afraid that he might be caught and fined, called across, "Mister, you had better stop smoking. Do you see that sign? It says you're not allowed to smoke."

"So?" replied the old man. "Over there is a sign that says 'EAT CORN FLAKES.' So does that mean I gotta eat corn flakes?"

A proud resident was taking an old friend for a tour of the Bronx. To his visiting pal he pointed out an imposing building and identified it as an orphans' home.

"Now, Hymie," said his old friend. "Personally I happen to know that's not an orphan asylum, but it's an old man's home."

"All right. But if you go inside I'll bet you won't find one old man who isn't an orphan."

Eli and Bessie went to sleep. In the middle of the night, Bessie nudged Eli.

"Please, Eli, be so kindly and close the window. It's so cold outside!"

Half asleep, Eli murmured, "Nu...so if I'll close the window, will it be warm outside?"

Oppenheimer, a stock broker, was a devout Jew. He became seriously ill and his friends learned his days might be numbered. His cronies from the synagogue came to visit him, perhaps for the last time. His closest friend, Mr. Lipsky, stayed on after the others had left.

Oppenheimer said, "Well, my dear friend, I guess it's pretty close to the end. Otherwise, would all our shule friends come so hurriedly to pay their respects?"

"You're talking nonsense," consoled Lipsky. "With your constitution, you'll live to be ninety! God will see to that."

"What do you think, God can't figure things out mathematically? If he can get me at seventy-four, why should he wait until ninety?"

The employees of B. Rheinhardt and Company decided to have a weekly lottery, just to liven up their lives. The man who picked the lucky number won the jackpot.

For three weeks running, Hymie Fox had the lucky number. His compatriots couldn't figure out how Hymie did it. Was it just plain luck or did he have a method of figuring it?

At lunch, one of the boys said, "Hymie, how come you're the lucky one three weeks in a row?"

Another said, "Do you have some kind of a system?"

"It's simple," said Hymie. "I dream. The other night I saw eight sevens dancing before my eyes. Eight sevens are forty-eight so I figured forty-eight had to be the lucky number; so I picked it!"

"But Hymie, eight sevens are fifty-six, not forty-eight!"

"Nu!" answered Hymie. "So YOU be the mathematician!"

Many years ago, in Austria when Franz Joseph ruled the country, a kindly and revered rabbi and his driver used to drive from town to town to visit the townspeople, and conduct services. After the services, there was a feast. Then the lansman* would gather around the rabbi to ask questions and advice. His driver always sat off in the corner and ate alone.

This went on for many years. One day, the driver said to the rabbi, Reb Gedalia, "I have been your devoted driver for many years. I have listened as you answered wisely all sorts of questions. But always I have had to sit off in the corner by myself and eat by myself. Before I die, I would like to change places with you for just once. Just once, I would like a taste of what it is to be admired and respected as you are."

The good rabbi laughed and said he would be happy to comply with his wish. They would naturally have to go to a community they had never visited before, someplace where they were not known. And so the rabbi and the driver changed clothes and drove many miles from their usual route so that the driver's wish might be realized.

The townspeople, as usual, gathered around after the services. There was a fine table spread and the driver, dressed as the rabbi, partook of the feast while the rabbi sat off in the corner eating by himself. The lansman began to ask all sorts of questions. The driver was well schooled by now and answered every question as well as the rabbi had always done.

But in the group, there was a young student who was anxious to show off his own knowledge. Instead of the usual type of question, he asked an involved and profound one that no one had ever asked in any of the other villages.

The driver said, "Young man, I am amazed that you should ask so simple a question. Why, even my driver who is not well-versed in the Talmud,* could answer you. And to prove it, we'll ask him!"

A young man lost his way in the Williamsburg section of Brooklyn. He stopped an old, venerable looking man, and became exasperated when the old man couldn't give him satisfactory directions.

"Don't you know anything?" he asked.

"Anyway, I know where *I* am," was the sage answer.

Two dress manufacturers met in a dairy restaurant in the garment district. After inquiring about each other's health, the first asked, "So how is business?"

The second answered with a shrug and a grunt, "Ehhh!"

"For this time of the year, with the season almost over, that's not bad!"

---

*Lansman—*townspeople*
*Talmud—*sacred writing*

Two rabbis were having a philosophical discussion as they drank glass after glass of hot tea with lemon spiced with cloves.

The discussion over, they said "shalom" and each began to go his own way. But Reb Yankel called to his friend and said, "By the way, Reb Zacharia, I forgot to mention one thing. What do you think of one of our boys marrying that Elizabeth Taylor?"

"Ach, it wouldn't last a year!"

"A zar yure uff mir!"* murmured Reb Yankel.

*In Yiddish—"*I should have such a year*"

Pasquale and Itzick worked as pressers in a mens' clothing factory. They shared each other's companionship during coffee breaks and lunch, which they ate in the factory. They became good friends.

One day they began philosophizing about how fortunate they were to be in America.

Pasquale said, "Yes, Itzick, we were so poor, we lived practically on vegetables which we grew. We hardly ever had a piece of meat or fish...that's how poor we were, in the town we lived in in Italy!"

Itzick replied, "You think you had it bad! We were practically starving all the time. And to make matters worse, our village which was outside of Siberia, was like one big icicle for most of the year. Believe me, if it wasn't for central heating, we'd have all frozen to death!"

"You mean you were so poor and your house had central heating?"

"Not our house! We! All winter we lived on grated horse-radish with chicken fat and for a change, fried potato lotkiss.* From this, we had perpetual heartburn which kept us warm in those severe Russian winters!"

*Lotkiss—*Pancakes*

There was great jubilation in the little dry goods store on Pitkin Avenue in Brooklyn! The Resnikoffs' son Larry had just graduated from Harvard Business School and had made fine grades. Before going off to conquer Wall Street and the rest of the world, he had promised to do what he could to systematize and expand papa's business.

"One of the first things we'll do is get an accountant to straighten things out. When bills come in, you just stick them in the cookie jar. Every once in a while, you take them out of the cookie jar, take money out of the cash register and pay them. You've got to keep a set of books! How do you expect to ever really build this business up into another Macy's? But don't worry, Dad, we'll get you a combination of an efficiency expert and accountant and you'll see...we'll wind up on the Big Board!"

The accountant spent several days in the store, huddled with Mr. Resnikoff. He left and submitted a handsome bill for his services. Mrs. Resnikoff noticed that her husband seemed very worried and started to question him. He tried to avoid any discussion but finally blurted out that the accountant informed him that he was practically bankrupt!

"Yes, Sonia, I'm so worried that I haven't even been sleeping. I don't know where to turn!"

The wise Sonia said, "Listen to me, Pincus. We've always had what to eat, yes? A roof also we always had over our heads, no? We sent our Larry not only to Cornell but also to Harvard Business School too, yes? The store is the same; you and me are the same; and our customers, thank God, are also the same. Only the accountant is different! So, I have a simple solution! Let's send away the accountant!"

A Cleveland Jew, on his first trip to New York, headed for the United Nations in which he was keenly interested.

In one of the lounges, he was startled to come upon an ancient looking man, the oldest he had ever seen in his life. His bearing and appearance seemed to be of another world. The American's curiosity was aroused. He decided to engage him in conversation. He walked over to him. After the usual amenities were disposed of, the American asked where the old man was from.

"I am from Palestine. I have lived there all of my very long life. I decided before I die, I would like to see America, so here I am!"

"I notice you say 'very long life.' Would you think me bold if I asked how old you are?"

"Not at all, my son. I'm sure you will be startled to learn that I am almost two thousand years old!"

21

"'Startled' is an understatement! Two thousand years old! How could that be?" asked the American.

"How could it be, you ask? It is!"

This all seemed incredible but after all this patriarchal old Jew looked quite ancient.

"If you are almost two thousand years old and you lived in Palestine, could you possibly have known Jesus?"

"Yes, I met him when he was a little boy."

"I'm very much interested! Could you tell me about it?" queried the American.

"I'd be glad to. You see, young man, I was a silversmith in Bethlehem. I made silver Stars of David. I worked very hard and barely eked out an existence. This was in the days long before soldering equipment was ever heard of. I had to fashion by hand six strips of silver. I then had to join two sets of triangles, insert one on top of the other in order to make one Star of David. And in the final analysis, after laboring so long and hard, there was not much of a market for my work. One day, this little boy, Jesus, came into my shop and watched as I worked. He began to speak to me and I listened. Do you know what this young boy said? He suggested that instead of making those difficult stars, why didn't I just take two silver strips, one long and one short, and just lay the shorter strip part way down across the longer strip. He insisted that I would not have to work so hard and I could sell millions of these and make a fortune!"

"He said all that to you? Well, what did you do?"

"What did I do?" muttered the old man, shaking his head sadly. "I chased him from my shop, admonishing him not to bother me, that I was too busy to listen to his foolishness!"

"Well, why did you do that?" asked the young man.

"Gay vace!"*

The old man lay dying and his friend sat at his bedside. The friend could see that his days were numbered.

"You've been a pious man all your life, Meyer. Would you like me to call the rabbi so that you can make your peace with God?"

"I was not aware that we quarrelled," answered Meyer.

In a small town in Galicia, Poland, a poor man came running to Reb Zachariah for advice.

"Rabbi, please help me! I'm in serious trouble. I have a wife and eight children, three boys and five girls, to support. I do not make enough money to feed a family half the size. Yet every year, my wife presents me with a new child! Advise me, Rabbi, what shall I do?"

"Do? Take my advice, do nothing!" was the sage retort.

---

*Who could be so smart?

PROBLEMS:
OR IT SHOULDN'T
HAPPEN TO A DOG

Mendel owned some land in the Catskills as well as some cows. He decided to build a small hotel. He had visions of some day developing it into another Grossinger's. But there was one thing wrong: business was terrible!

He was about to close the hotel and take his loss when a friend from New York City came to visit him. Mendel confided his troubles to him.

"All right," said his old friend. "So you can't make a go of running a hotel, so forget about it. But you have good land for your cows to graze on. And you have beautiful Golden Guernseys and Holsteins. Why don't you cross-breed them? There's a fortune to be made in cross-breeding. What have you got to lose?"

Mendel agreed that it was worth a try.

A year went by and Mendel came to New York City to visit his friend.

"So, how did you make out with the cows?"

"Oy!" answered Mendel. "For everything you gotta have luck! I did like you said and cross-bred the Golden Guernsey with a Holstein. From it I got a beautiful Goldstein but nobody wanted to buy it!"

"Why?"

"Why, you ask? When a customer looked at the other cows, the cows said, 'Moooooooo'; when the customer looked at my Goldstein, he said, 'Nuuuuuuuuuu'!"

Two old chess players stopped their game in Central Park and commiserated with each other about the disadvantages of advancing age.

"Yes," said the elder of the two, "I now chase girls only when it's downhill!"

Two elderly Jewish scholars sat drinking glass of tea after glass of tea without saying a word. After two hours of silence, Yankel said, "You know, Moishe, life is like a bowl of cherries!"

"Why, Yankel?"

"Why," he's asking me. "What am I, a philosopher?"

Two neighbors ran into each other in Paris.

"How are things?" said the first.

Her friend answered in a distressed tone, "Oy, I've been here three days already and I haven't been to the Louvre yet!"

"You know what?" said the other. "Me, too...it must be the water!"

A half hour after an El Al plane left Idlewild, the control tower was startled to receive a message from the pilot that the plane was headed back to Idlewild.

The tower relayed a hurried message to the pilot.

"Are you in trouble?"

"I sure am! We forgot the pickles!"

The ladies were sunning themselves in the solarium. One very garrulous lady started to talk about her analyst.

"Why he's marvelous! You ought to go to him!"

"But my dear," said her burned-to-a-crisp neighbor, "why do you suggest such a thing to me? There's nothing wrong with me!"

"You don't understand. He's so wonderful...he'll find something!"

The star salesman of the Adorable Dress Company had one fault; he was known to occasionally take one drink too many. He did bring in the business and so this shortcoming was overlooked.

One morning, the salesman's wife 'phoned to say that her husband would not be in that day. He had slipped on ice the night before.

The boss said, "Tell him to take care of himself. By the way, tell him I asked how in the devil he got his big foot into that highball glass!"

Mrs. Mefoofsky seemed very depressed and her husband wanted to know what was troubling her.

"I'm the only one in my whole canasta club who doesn't have a fur coat. I have to walk around in a crummy cloth coat. Before you know it, people will begin to think we're Republicans!"

That did it!

"Before that, here's a hundred dollars and go buy a fur coat!"

She pleaded a hundred dollars was not nearly enough.

"Whatya mean 'not enough?' I see beautiful fur coats advertised in the Daily News for $99! My final word is take it or leave it!"

And so dejectedly she took it, went to Klein's and bought a black mouton coat.

The following week, they went to the theatre. She sat there with her mouton coat folded on her lap. A woman came down the aisle with a gorgeous ranch mink coat draped over her shoulders.

Mrs. Mefoofsky nudged her husband and said dejectedly, "See that's the kind of fur coat I really wanted."

"So," he said. "If you wanted brown, why did you buy black?"

A little Jewish boy said to his mother, "Mama, I'm trying so hard to learn to speak Jewish but I find it so confusing. I find that two words sometimes mean the samething!"

"Give me a for instance?"

"All right! Isn't a shlemiel*[1] the same as a shlamazel*[2]?"

"There's a big difference! The shlemiel is the one that drops a plate of hot soup into the lap of the shlamazel!"

Julius Feitelbaum walked into a German delicatessen and asked the clerk for a pound of potato salad and a pound of cole slaw.

Pointing to the Virginia Ham, he said, "How much is that smoked meat a pound?"

Before the clerk could answer, there was a deafening clap of thunder that practically shook the whole store and its occupants. Feitelbaum looked up and pleaded, "Alright, God Almighty, I was only asking!"

---

*[1]—Shlemiel—*Yiddish for a clumsy one.*
*[2]—Shlamazel—*Yiddish for a misfortunate one.*

25

The Pussywillow Golf Club had one of the most beautiful and challenging courses in Westchester. It also had a restricted membership policy.

Jake Schwartz was an excellent golfer who had played on championship courses in all parts of the country. He was determined to play the Pussywillow course even if it was restricted to Gentiles only. He changed his name from Jake Schwartz to Jonathan Black. He took elocution lessons to remove all traces of his Jewish accent. He went to a plastic surgeon and had his nose bobbed. He was sure no one at the club would recognize him as a Jew. He applied for membership and was admitted.

His friend drove him to the club and warned him something would happen before the day ended. Jake said, "With my new name, my new accent, my new nose and everything else new, how can they tell I'm Jewish?"

His friend decided to wait anyway. An hour later, a set of golf clubs, a traveling bag, clothes and Jonathan Black (nee Jake Schwartz) were thrown out through the club house door.

His friend said, "What happened?"

"Oh," said Jake. "Everything was fine. But there's a small lake to the left of the third fairway. When I hooked my drive into the lake, the waters parted!"

Two women ran into each other on Collins Avenue in Miami Beach. They hadn't seen each other in years and were obviously pleased to meet again.

The younger woman said, "So how are you feeling, dolling?"

"Oy, not so good! I feel terrible! That's why I just flew down to Miami!"

Disturbed, her friend inquired, "Have you been through the menapause yet?"

"The Menapause?...I haven't been through the Fountainbleau yet!"

Two men were huddled next to each other in a crowded subway train. All of a sudden they recognized each other. They used to play together when they were kids on the lower East Side. In fact both their fathers had been pushcart peddlers on Orchard Street; one sold shirts, the other notions. And both the boys had helped their fathers after school.

"Gee! Imagine meeting you after all these years!" said Itzick. "And how is your father?"

"He got wiped out in the 1929 crash!"

"You mean from peddling notions, he made enough money to play the stock market?"

"Heck no! Some stockbroker jumped out of the window and fell on him!"

Moe was looking through the want-ads. His friend asked:

"Hey, ain't you working at the Kosher Kracker Company any more?"

"Naw! I got fired for slipping in pigs in the animal crackers!"

The wealthiest Jew in Great Neck died and all his friends and relatives gathered to pay their last respects. There were many cars in the funeral procession and many people walked behind the cars in tribute to the memory of the great philanthropist. One man was sighing deeply and was seen wiping away a tear or two.

"You must be a close relative of the deceased," a woman asked in a sympathetic voice.

"I'm not related to him at all!"

"Then why are you crying?"

"That's why!"

Right after they installed parking meters on Pitkin Avenue in Brooklyn, two dogs out for their constitutional, stopped in amazement.

"What-ya-know," the poodle remarked to the cocker, "Pay toilets!"

Lapidus was the type of faithful husband who never went out with the boys. He was beginning to feel he was missing something. One night at supper, he brought up the subject.

Fanny said, "So why don't you go? It wouldn't hurt you to play a little pinochle with the boyiss!"

When the fellows in the shop mentioned their night on the town the following week, he said, "Boyiss, today I'm a regular Johnny-on-the-spot! So where do you play pinochle, here in shop or in somebody's parlor?"

The boys howled with laughter.

"Ladipdus," one of them said. "We play but it aint pinochle."

He consented to tag along, assuring himself that it was only because he was a good sport.

Several days later, he began to feel a little peculiar. Without a word to anyone, he went to see his doctor. He learned the bad news. He was terribly upset and decided to tell all to Fanny. He reasoned if he confessed the truth, God would forgive him and make him better. After dinner that night, he said, "Fanny dolling, sit down. I have something to tell you."

"So I'm sitting, so tell me already."

He said sadly, "Fanny dolling, I'm very upset and I want you should forgive me. I think I picked up a case of gonorrhea!"

"What's to forgive? I think it'll be a nice change from Manischewitz!"

A car stopped short at a gas station. Mrs. Hirsch jumped out looking rather uncomfortable. She glanced about, hoping to find a ladies' room but couldn't seem to find one.

She approached the attendant and said, "I beg your pardon, but do you have a ladies' waiting room?"

"No, ma'am," answered the wise-guy, "but we have a room for ladies who can't wait!"

A pious Jew and a known sinner were travelling to America on an ocean liner.

A terrible storm came up and the ship began rocking mercilessly. Word began to spread that their ship was in danger of sinking. Everyone on the ship began to pray, including the crew. As the pious Jew was praying, he noticed that the sinner had broken down and was praying as well. He stopped his own praying and nudged him.

"Sh-sh," pleaded the pious one, "Don't let God know you are here or it will be the end of all of us!"

A young bachelor assured his mother he was going to synagogue on Yom Kippur, the holiest day of the year.

Instead, he sneaked into the basement of his home, changed his clothes and went off to play golf.

He had never played so well! In fact, for the first time in his life, he made a hole in one.

He was elated...but not for long. Suddenly, he heard a voice from Heaven:

"All right, wise-guy, so whom can you tell this to?"

A psychiatrist received a card from one of his patients vacationing in Miami Beach:

"Having a wonderful time! Wish you were here to tell me why!"

Upon graduation from college, Melvin Teitelbaum announced to his parents he did not want to go into papa's business. For years, he had dreamed of becoming an actor and now he wanted to have a try at it. His parents were quite unhappy about it but decided if it meant their son's happiness, they would give in.

He went off to New York City and enrolled in a drama school. After three years, he finally managed to get a part in a play on Broadway. The New York critics panned it mercilessly and it closed after three days. But the producers were determined to try again and the show went on tour. Melvin wrote home that their home town, Chicago, was included in the tour.

The Teitelbaums bought tickets for the whole family, all their friends and even their distant cousins for opening night. This was to be Melvin's big day!

At last the curtain went up. Mama and papa were on

tenterhooks waiting for Melvin's appearance. The first act passed. There was no sign of Melvin.

The second act passed. Mama and papa were perspiring. Still no Melvin.

The third act. Still no Melvin. Just before the final curtain came down, out came Melvin, gun in hand, made up to look like an old-type Chicago gangster. He made menacing motions with the gun but did not utter a word!

This was too much for Mrs. Teitelbaum! She was bitter about such humiliating treatment of her son. Just as the curtain was coming down, she lost all control and shouted, "For God's sake, Melvin, if they don't let you talk—at least shoot!"

Max Cohen was an observant Jew, a bachelor who lived alone. He found it a little lonesome and decided to buy a parrot to keep him company. Every morning before going off to work, he put on his prayer shawl and chanted his morning prayer in lusty tones.

One morning, he was startled to hear his parrot recite the prayer after him. Each morning thereafter, after Max finished his prayers, the parrot chanted his. Max was so amused that he named him Moishe Goniff. Max told his poker cronies about his remarkable bird. They howled with laughter and said they didn't believe him. Max bet them fifty dollars his parrot could recite the Hebrew prayer.

The following week was Rosh Hashonah. He invited his friends to come to his house after services and he would convince them and thus win his bet.

After the services, they gathered at Max's house. Max told the parrot to chant the prayer. The bird remained silent. Max then recited the prayer and expected the parrot would repeat it. The parrot did not utter a sound. His friends kidded him and poor Max had to pay off. When his friends left, Max rushed to the cage and screamed, "Moishe Goniff! I buy you the best parrot food money can buy! I even bought you a gold cage! How could you double-cross me like this?"

"What are you getting so excited for?" answered Moishe Goniff. "Why should I bother for a lousy fifty bucks! Look at the odds you can get for me now to sing on Yom Kippur!"

Abie and Raizel went to City Hall for a wedding license. They were told at the information desk to go to the second floor, fill out forms, take them to the fifth floor where the license would be issued.

The man behind the cage on the fifth floor started to read the form and said, "Abie is not your real name. Isn't it Abraham? Go back to the second floor, fill out the form correctly and bring it back here."

They returned in a little while and handed in the new form. The man began to read. His name was correctly spelled but when he came to "Raizel Mintz," he said, "Is that your English name? It sounds like a foreign name."

"My English name is 'Rose' but since Abie calls me by my Jewish name, I thought it would be alright to put it down like that."

"I'm sorry, these forms have to be filled out in English! Go back to the second floor, fill out a new form and bring it back here."

They returned once more.

He began to read. The names were alright now. The address was listed as 128 East New York Ave., Brownsville, N.Y.

"Brownsville, N.Y.? Brownsville is just a section of Brooklyn. You have to write 'Brooklyn, N.Y.' not 'Brownsville.' Go back to the second floor, fill out the form correctly and bring it back to me."

They returned to the fifth floor, and limply handed it through the cage. The man perused it and said, "Well, at last everything is o.k. now. Three dollars please and you may have your license."

He handed the license to Abie who turned to Raizel and said, "You know, Raizel. Some day our little boy will be glad we made everything legal."

The man in the cage said, "Did I hear you say you two have a little boy?"

"Yeah," answered Abie. "He was born last week!"

"You already have a baby and you're just getting a wedding license today? Do you know that makes your little boy a technical bastard?"

"So?" shrugged Abie, "You're doing all right, ain't you? And that's what the man on the second floor said you are!"

The salesman was having a hard time. Every time he thought he had the mink coat sold, the customer threw in another monkey wrench.

At last, he thought he was about to close the deal.

"There's only one thing, Mr. Fink, what if I buy it and I'm caught in the rain? Will it be ruined?"

"Look, lady" he said disgustedly, "Did you ever see a mink carrying an umbrella?"

At a Bar Mitzvah reception, Mrs. Cantor and Mrs. Levy met after not seeing each other since they were both young girls in the Bronx.

They kissed and began to gossip about the good old days. All of a sudden, the lights were dimmed and the ceremony for the lighting of the candles on the large birthday cake began.

After the Bar Mitzvah boy lit the first candle, each of his friends was called upon to light the additional candles. As the third candle was being lit, Mrs. Cantor turned to her friend and said, "Oy! Look at that boy! A face, so full of pimples, you could throw up looking at him!"

"Please!" bristled Mrs. Levy, "It so happens that he's my boy, Bruce!"

"Darling!" gushed her friend, "You know what? On him, the pimples are becoming!"

Mr. Lowenberg was in the hospital for observation. Every morning, he was served the same breakfast. The tray contained a glass of apple juice, toast, two soft boiled eggs, tea and an empty urinal bottle.

After breakfast, he was visited by a "we" nurse, the kind who always says, "And how are 'we' feeling this morning? And did 'we' have a good night's sleep? And did 'we' remember to take care of our specimen this morning?" ad infinitum.

The routine began to get on his nerves.

The next morning, he was determined to play tricks. When the tray was brought in, he ate the toast, the two soft boiled eggs, and drank the tea. He then poured the apple juice into the urinal bottle and waited.

The nurse breezed in.

"And how are 'we' feeling this morning? Ah, I see 'we' were a good boy and ate our whole breakfast!"

She glanced at the full urinal bottle.

"Well!" she added, "I guess 'we' weren't such a good boy after all! You must have done something you shouldn't have last night. I see the specimen is very cloudy this morning!"

Lowenberg picked up the urinal bottle, began to drink it while the 'we' nurse looked on in horror, and cracked, "Don't you think 'we' ought to run it through a second time!"

When the lodge meeting broke up, Meyer confided to a friend.

"Abe, I'm in a terrible pickle! I'm strapped for cash and I haven't the slightest idea where I'm going to get it from!"

"I'm glad to hear that" answered Abe. "I was afraid you might have an idea you could borrow it from me!"

31

Goldman's Mountainview House of the Catskills was a dismal failure. Goldman was just about to put a padlock on the door and write the whole thing off as a tax loss. His accountant suggested he call in an efficiency expert. Perhaps he could suggest something that might salvage his dying business.

A young man from a Madison Avenue firm was dispatched to the Catskills. He poured over the books, inspected the hotel and looked over the grounds. The only flaw he could find was the name of the resort hotel.

"I find the hotel quite attractive, Mr. Goldman. I would suggest, however, that you change the name. How can you expect to draw a young crowd to a place with a name like Goldman's Mountainview House of the Catskills? I would suggest a nice short, snappy name."

"All right, so we'll change the name. You have maybe a nice name in mind?"

The young man thought a moment and said, "How about 'Westward-Ho'?"

"So let it be already 'Westward-Ho'...anything so I wouldn't lose mine shirt!"

And so a new neon sign was made, new stationery ordered and the bus repainted with large bold letters which read "Westward-Ho." Goldman said to his Negro driver, "Everything is all set, Jackson, so you'll go down to meet the next train with the new bus and see what you can do!".

Jackson went down to the railroad station and brought back a whole bus load of young people. Goldman could scarcely believe his eyes! Elated, he said, "Good boy, Jackson, meet all the trains and if our luck continues like this, we'll be in business again!"

Each time Jackson met a train, he returned with the bus loaded. Finally, there wasn't a room left in the hotel and Goldman turned to Jackson and said, "Ach, you're wonderful! What did you do to get all these guests to come to our hotel?"

"Ah didn't do nothin' boss," said Jackson. "I jest stood beside the bus and yelled out 'This way to the Westward Ho-House'!"

At the weekly bridge game, Sophie seemed rather glum and distracted. One of her friends noticed this and asked if anything was wrong.

Sophie explained that she might have to get rid of her French poodle whom she dearly loved. The dog had suddenly become very nervous, was constantly barking and the neighbors were complaining. One of her friends was very sympathetic.

"Sophie, don't you know they now have dog psychiatrists? Why don't you take Poochie to him? He might straighten him out?"

"It would never work," said Sophie disconsolately, "From the time he was a puppy, I trained him to keep off couches!"

Nathan was walking along Delancey Street, swaying along with his arm rounded out, his hand resting on his hip. He ran into Izzy who looked at him suspiciously.

"Nathan, for twenty years already I know you and respected you. What's with you...all of a sudden, you're walking like a 'faigelle!' What heppened to you?"

"What heppened to me?" Looking down towards his arm, he yelled, "Beckey will kill me! I lost my pumpernickel!"

A man walked into a little shop on Canal Street on the lower East Side. As the door opened, a loud bell clanked and an elderly Jewish man, wearing the traditional skull cap, emerged from the back of the store.

"I can maybe help you?" asked the old man.

"My watch just stopped. I see you sell watches. Do you also repair them?"

"Who told you I sell watches? Didn't you see on the window, it says 'J. Radustovitch—Mohel'?"*

"Well," said the young man, "If you're a mohel, why do you have watches in your window?"

"You can suggest, maybe, something better I can put in the window?" replied the old man.

Two accountants were having lunch. They had been friends since their school days and their weekly lunch date had become a ritual.

"What's the matter, Stanley, you seem to be upset about something?"

"Well, I'm not really upset. I'm annoyed. My wife told me that she dreamt last night she had married a multi-millionaire!"

"Boy, you're lucky," sighed his friend, "My wife dreams that in the daytime!"

---

*Mohel—*A man who performs circumcisions according to Rabbinic rite.*

33

The steam room in the Turkish bath was crowded and foggy. Through the mist, Abe thought he recognized an old friend whom he hadn't seen in over ten years. Jake, too, seemed overjoyed at meeting an old lansman*. After being wrapped in sheets, they lay side by side reminiscing happily.

Abe said, "Didn't you have a son, Marvin?"

"Oy, have I a son, Marvin! And do I have trouble from mine Marvin! He graduated from Harvard. So when he got out, what could he do besides cheer? Nothing! So, foolishly, I took him into the business. He comes in at ten in the morning, goes out to lunch at 11, stays out 'till two. Two o'clock, he comes back, goes in the showroom, fools around with the models until four, then he goes home to Scarsdale. That's what pleasure I have from mine Marvin!"

Abe shook his head sadly, "You think you got tsuriss*. Oy, don't complain. I'm the one with A-number-one troubles, a hundred times worse than yours. Remember I had a boy, Stevie, the same age as your Marvin? So I put him through Princeton. What could he do when he finished? Also nothing. So also like you, I took him into the business. He comes in at ten. He goes out to lunch at eleven, stays out 'till two, comes back, goes into the showroom, fools around with the models 'till four. Four o'clock, he runs for his train to Great Neck!"

Jake raged, "What's with you? You tell me you got worse troubles and then you tell me the same eyedentical story what I just told you!"

"Mine dear friend," said Abe sadly, "You forget, I'm in *men's* clothing!"

The Bornsteins owned a candy store on Hester Street. They worked seven days a week from early morning until late at night. They had one daughter, Rachel, and they were determined she would have every advantage they had never enjoyed.

Upon graduation from high school, Rachel went off to college. Everything was fine the first year. She wrote home every week and her grades were fair. In the middle of the semester of her sophomore year, she appeared in the candy store.

Poppa said, "Ray, whatya' doing home in the middle of the term? It's a special holiday maybe?"

"Pop, I have bad news for you! I'm going to have a baby!"

Poppa grabbed his head with both hands and wailed, "She's gonna' have a baby! For this momma and I had to save and scrimp and work our fingers to the bone! And she comes home and tells me she's gonna' have a baby!"

Rachel said, "Gee, honestly, Pop, I'm sorry! But

that's the way it is! Getting hysterical isn't going to help."

This had a calming effect and he figured he had better get down to specifics. He asked, "All right, Ray, so who's the father?"

"I don't know, Pop. Honestly, I just don't know!"

Poppa flew into a rage.

"She just don't know! We sent you off to college. All right, a genius we didn't expect they'd make out of you! But a little simple manners, I thought they'd teach you. Whatsa matter, you couldn't say, 'You shull be so kindly, but with whom am I having the pleasure?' "

In 1942, Saperstein and Finkelstein had been partners and good friends for years. They had worked hard and their men's clothing business prospered.

Saperstein noticed that his partner was getting thinner and greyer and learned that he had been running from doctor to doctor. They had a heart-to-heart talk and Finkelstein admitted he had become an insomniac. His visits to the doctors had been of no avail!

"So why don't you try the simplest and oldest remedy of all? Long before tranquilizers were on the market, people who couldn't sleep counted sheep and it worked! So what have you got to lose?"

In desperation, Finkelstein said he'd try it that very night. The next morning, he came in looking more haggard than before.

"I thought I told you to try counting sheep!" chided Saperstein.

"Oy! don't ask!" moaned his friend. "I did like you said. Then my troubles really started! I counted up to 10,000 sheep! So what do you do with 10,000 sheep? Have them sheared, naturally! It made beautiful bolts of cloth, from which I had made up 10,000 garments. The garments hung on the racks and I suddenly remembered. "Oy! with the war still on and silk hard to get, where in the world could I get 10,000 linings!"

---

*Lansman—*In Yiddish, a man born in the same town.*
*Tsuriss—*In Yiddish, trouble.*

35

Isaac Tannenbaum had come to this country penniless. An old friend from a neighboring town in Galicia had generously loaned him two hundred dollars. With the money, he purchased needles, pins and other notions so he could start a peddling business.

But times were hard and he just couldn't seem to scrape together the money to pay off the debt. He was a man of good conscience and this began to bother him.

One night, his wife awoke in the middle of the night and found him pacing the floor.

"Why are you walking up and down like you were maybe expecting me to give birth any minute?" queried Sarah.

"I'm so worried I can't sleep and you're making jokes! God knows when I'll be able to pay back my good friend, Yankel, the two hundred dollars!"

"Fool! Go back better to sleep. If that's the case, let Yankel walk the floor, not you!"

A blinding blizzard was raging! The snow was so deep as to make walking impossible. All the stores in the neighborhood were closed for no one would dare venture out in the storm.

Mr. Kaminsky turned out the lights in his little grocery store. In the room in back of the store, he lit his little stove and drank glass after glass of hot tea to keep warm.

All of a sudden, he heard a terrific pounding on his front door! He hesitated to answer but figured it could only be a grave emergency to bring someone out in such weather.

Hesitantly, he opened the door and in staggered Pincus Rippsky! He wore two sweaters, a jacket, an overcoat, and a hat with earlaps. Over his shoes, he had galoshes, wrapped in burlap bags! He was frozen stiff and his teeth chattered so that he could not open his mouth to speak!

"Mr. Rippsky, what are you doing out on a day like this? Even a dog wouldn't stick out his nose! What can I do for you?"

Rippsky stammered, "I want only two seeded rolls."

"Two seeded rolls!", Kaminsky gasped! "You mean for this, your wife sent you out?"

"Who then?" dejectedly answered Rippsky, "My mother?"

Mrs. Eisenstein's extravagant ways were getting on her husband's nerves.

After dinner, she announced, "Darling, I was at the doctor's today and he ordered a change in climate!"

"Fine!" he retorted. "According to the weather girl on TV, it's coming tomorrow!"

Sam Kracow had been a loving and faithful husband to Molly for twenty years. He worked in a dress factory as a cutter and ate lunch with his fellow-workers. They sat around the long cutting table eating the lunches their wives had prepared and drank coffee from their thermos bottles. And they talked.

Every once in a while, one of his friends would boast of an extra-marital affair. Sam would listen silently. He had nothing to brag about except his children's good grades in school. He began to feel cheated. He made a rash decision. He would go to one of those houses just once. Then he too could be a "big-shot!" One of the fellows gave him an address.

With trepidation and some embarrassment, he asked for a woman. To lessen his guilt, he mumbled that she needn't be young or beautiful...a nice comfortable woman would do.

He was told to go into a room down the hall. In a few minutes, after first knocking gently at the door, a woman entered. She was middle-aged, plump, with a sweet face devoid of make-up except for a little lipstick. Shyly, he said, "Hello! My name is Sam Kracow. What's yours?"

"Emma Epstein!"

He was taken aback! His face reddened...and he was even more embarrassed now than when he had entered the house. He blurted out, "You know, I've never been in a place like this before!"

She answered sweetly, "You know what? Neither have I!"

"What do you mean...neither have you? So what are you doing here?"

"Well, you see it's like this...I was seventeen dollars shy on my Sisterhood pledge!"

In the maternity ward of a hospital in Israel, a student nurse walked from bed to bed, asking questions and making notations on her chart.

She spoke to an occupant of one of the beds.

"Good morning! I understand your baby was born during the night. Mazel tov*! Have you decided on a name for the baby for we'd like to record it?"

"Yes...I want to call him 'Nasser'!"

Shocked, the nurse repeated, "Nasser? Are you serious?"

"I was never more serious in all my life!"

"This is a democracy and you are free to name him whatever you wish. But are you sure, Mrs. Rubinstein, that that's the name you wish?"

"Yes, I'm sure! And by the way, nurse, it's *Miss* Rubinstein, not *Mrs.* Rubinstein!"

Jewish phrase for "Good luck."

37

After the monthly meetings of the Mespocheh Benevolent Society, the "boys" would play pinochle and drink kosher wine. It was good getting together without their wives and they looked forward to these bi-monthly sessions.

There was one jarring note, however. Max, a quiet enough looking fellow, drank until he passed out cold. Someone had to take him home and the festivities would end on a sour note.

The president of the society warned him to drink in moderation next time or be expelled. He promised. At the next meeting, Max forgot his promise and again passed out.

Abe, the president, decided there was only one way to cure him.

"Let's take him to the cemetery and leave him there. That should cure him for good!"

And so they picked poor Max up, drove him out to the cemetery and laid him on the grass on the Society's burial plot...and left. The next morning, Max awoke, opened his eyes and closed them again in horror. Confused, he muttered to himself, "If I'm alive, what am I doing here laid out among the tombstones? And if I'm dead, how come I gotta' go to the bathroom?"

LAUGHING WITH TEARS IN MY EYES

When Harry S. Truman was our president, Chaim Weizmann, the first president of Israel visited him at the White House.

Over lunch, they commiserated with each other about the trials and tribulations facing the president of a country.

President Truman said, "I know you have many problems, with thousands of new immigrants pouring in. I know too that your country is in dire financial straits. But how can you compare your problems with mine? You have about two million people while I have over one hundred and twenty million!"

"Ah, Mr. President," replied Mr. Weizmann, "It's true you are the president of one hundred and twenty million people. But remember, I am the president of two million presidents!"

A Jewish soldier stationed in Germany decided on his day off, to browse around an old Jewish cemetery in Berlin. He read the various tombstones with interest.

All of a sudden, he was startled to come across a magnificent mausoleum on which was etched the famous name of ROTHSCHILD. He mused over the beauty and costliness of the enormous tombstone and murmured, "Boy! That's what I call living!"

Little Michael ran home from school all excited!

His patriarchal grandfather sat sipping a glass of tea as he read the Talmud.

"Gee grandpa! Guess what! Mickey Mantle hit three homers today!"

"Tell me, son, your Mickey Mantle...is what he did good for the Jews?"

In a writing class at the Sorbonne, the professor asked each student to write a story about a horse. It could deal with any aspect providing the central theme dealt with a horse.

The French student wrote about "The Love Life of a Horse."

The English student wrote of "Horse-racing, the Sport of Kings."

The American student wrote of "The Cost and Up-keep of a Horse."

And the Jewish student wrote of "The Horse and Anti-Semitism."

Nikita Khrushchev was afraid that Stalin's many followers might start a rebellion. One way to keep the memory of Stalin out of the minds of the Russian people was to get rid of the body. The dead dictator had been lying in state in the Kremlin.

He offered the body to France. DeGaulle declined. He gave a good reason. He thought Stalin's body placed on public view would detract from one of the sightseeing landmarks in Paris...Napoleon's tomb.

Khrushchev then offered Stalin's body to England. Prime Minister Macmillan graciously declined. He said, "We have to save the state burial space for our number one statesman, Sir Winston Churchill."

Khrushchev then offered the body of Stalin to Israel. He told Mr. Ben-Gurion that since relations between their two governments had been less than cordial, this gesture might lead to a better understanding. Prime Minister Ben-Gurion gladly accepted. The Israeli Prime Minister told the Soviet Premier, "We consider it an honor to accept the offer of the Soviet Republic and we will display Joseph Stalin's dead body. But I should warn you, this is a land noted for Resurrection!"

A large area of the Williamsburg section of Brooklyn is inhabited by Hasidim. They are easily recognizable. The men, and even the boys, wear black suits, long black coats, black bowler-type hats, beards and long side-curls.

They convert stores and small homes into houses of worship and there are many in the neighborhood. In fact, one street has so many of these little synagogues, that it is referred to as the "Rue de la Payess.*"

As if Castro were not having enough trouble with America's Get-Tough-Policy on Cuba, Prime Minister Ben-Gurion of Israel sent him the following cable:

IF YOU AIM ANY OF YOUR ROCKETS AT MIAMI BEACH, I WILL CONSIDER THIS AN ATTACK ON MY PEOPLE.

---

*Payess—*Jewish for side-curls worn by ultra-orthodox sects.*

Two neighbors were discussing a third neighbor whom they considered fanatic in his religiosity.

"Oh, him!" scoffed the neighbor, "He's so religious that on the High Holidays, he insists upon wearing stained glass in his eye-glasses!"

Molly Birnbaum joined the Peace Corps and was assigned to Africa.

Momma let her go reluctantly after many warnings and much maternal instruction.

Mail arrived regularly with glowing reports of her activities. One year later, Momma received a letter from Molly announcing she had married a doctor and was returning home with him.

Momma was beside herself with joy and she went to the pier to meet the ship. Molly was at the rail waving excitedly to Momma. Standing next to her was a seven foot African native. He carried a spear, wore a headdress of colored feathers, and had large rings through his nose and ears!

Momma yelled up to Molly, "I always told you to marry a 'rich' doctor, not a 'witch' doctor!"

A chauffeur-driven Cadillac was riding through Rivington Street on the lower East Side of New York. The car came to a sudden stop when the driver realized he had run over a cat.

The screeching brakes brought a little old shriveled Jewish lady running into the street from her small grocery store. She began to wring her hands and wail when she realized that her cat had been run down and killed.

The man in the back of the Cadillac came out and began to apologize profusely.

"I assure you it was an accident. My chauffeur just didn't see the cat. I'll be glad to pay you anything you want or do anything you say to make it up to you!"

Through her tears, the little old lady sobbed, "You can catch maybe mice?"

During the Hitler reign of terror, an elderly Jew sat in a train quietly gazing out the window. Opposite him, sat a storm-trooper with a large dog.

Each time the Nazi spoke to his dog, he addressed him as "Moses."

The Jew tried to ignore the innuendoes but the Nazi persisted in calling "Moses," each time in a louder voice.

The old man could not contain himself any longer.

"What a pity your poor dog has a Jewish name!"

"Why?"

"Well, having a Jewish name these days is quite a handicap! Without it, he might go far! He might even stand a chance of becoming a storm-trooper!"

Two old cronies met in the street after not seeing each other for more than twenty years because the Diamonds had moved from the lower East Side. They shook hands warmly and began to inquire about each other's families.

Diamond said, "Jacobson, I'm very proud to tell you both my boys are a great success. Dick is a doctor with a beautiful office, does very well and lives on Sutton Place. My Marlon is a lawyer, a regular Clarence Darrow, and makes $50,000 a year after taxes. All my friends should do so well! And how about your son? What is he doing?"

Jacobson answered, "My boy, Norman, is a rabbi."

"A rabbi? What kind of work is that for a Jewish boy!"

Life was hard for the Slutskys in Poland. They had one son who was getting close to the age where he might be called up for military service. They managed somehow to scrape together enough money to send their young son to America.

Several years later, their Isaac came home for a visit. He was dressed in the latest American fashion. Gone were the severe long black coat, black bowler hat, side curls and beard!

Papa was shocked!

"Where is your beard? And where are your payellech*?"

"Papa, practically everybody goes clean-shaven in America."

"You keep the dietary laws, I hope?"

"Papa, I eat in restaurants mainly, and it's very difficult to observe the dietary laws in that case."

"I'm sure you keep the Sabbath though!"

"I'm sorry, papa! Very few people can in America."

His world shattered, the old man said, "Tell me, son, are you still circumcised?"

An elderly Jewish man was walking in Israel near the Syrian border. He noticed an Arab walking towards him with a handsome dog. The Jew greeted the Arab but the greeting was not returned.

Figuring that, perhaps, he had not heard the greeting, he remarked about the fine looking dog.

"What breed is he?" inquired the old man.

"Undoubtedly a cross between a Hebrew and a mongrel!"

"Ah," said the elderly Jew, "Then he is undoubtedly related to both of us!"

---

*Side-curls worn by an ultra-orthodox sect of Jews.

An Irishman, a Scotsman and a Jew were close friends. At about the same time, each began complaining of not feeling well. They discovered that they had the same symptoms. Since they were on in years and not too affluent, they decided that one would go to a doctor and the other two would share the expense of the visit and take the same medication. They drew lots and the Irishman won.

His friends waited outside to learn the panacea.

The Irishman emerged looking glum.

"My friends, I have bad news. We have only six months to live!"

A pall settled over them.

Suddenly, the Irishman said, "Well, I'm not gonna' spend my last months on earth looking like a funeral. I haven't seen my native Ireland in over thirty years. I'm gonna' book passage, visit my old cronies and make the most of every minute!"

The Scotsman shook his head and said, "Pal, you've given me an idea. I'll go back to Glasgow, look up my old relatives, go fishing and do all the things I did when I was a wee lad!"

The Jew replied, "Pat, you can go back to Ireland! Scotty, you can go back to Scotland! Me, I'm gonna' see a specialist!"

An American visitor to Israel saw Prime Minister Ben-Gurion among the spectators at a concert. During the intermission, the American approached him and they had a brief chat.

The Prime Minister said, "Since this is your first visit to our country, I'd be interested in hearing your impression of us."

The American was ecstatic; everything about the country was more wonderful than he had anticipated.

"But one thing baffles me, Mr. Prime Minister. I notice that everyone says 'shalom' for 'hello' and 'shalom' for 'goodbye!'"

"Well," said Mr. Ben-Gurion, "In our tiny democracy, we have so many problems that half the time, we don't know whether we're coming or going!"

In a little basement apartment in the Bronx, there was great jubilation! Ida had, at last, become pregnant! As the time approached, Ida became moody. Jake was worried and asked if anything was wrong.

Ida whined, "Jake dear, we're janitors but there's nothing we can do about that. But why, when my time will come, do the nurses in the hospital have to know? For once, I'd like people to think I'm a lady!"

Jake laughed and was relieved. "Ida dolling, I swear by all that's holy, I won't say a word!"

Ida became her old cheerful self again. When the time came, Jake rushed her to the hospital. At the hospital, they learned the birth was not as imminent as they had thought and the doctor suggested Jake go home, saying he'd be notified in due time.

Jake dragged himself home but lay awake. Early next morning, he received the good news! He was the father of a baby boy. He was overcome with joy. Without breakfast, he rushed into the nearest florist, bought a dozen roses and rushed to see his Ida! He burst into the room, was about to kiss her when she pushed him away, sobbing hysterically, "Go away from me! I never want to look on your face again! You didn't keep your promise!"

"Ida, mine doll! I was the happiest man in the world with a beautiful wife and now a son and you're pushing me away! What are you talking about? What promise didn't I keep?"

"I'll tell you," she wailed. "Early in the morning, the nurse came in. She looked at me with a sour face and her nose stuck up in the air and she said, 'Before I take your temperature, I want to know one thing . . . did you move the borrels this morning?' "

A young Negro girl returned home to Birmingham for a vacation. She had been working as a maid for a Jewish family in New York City. Relatives and friends wanted to know how she liked living in the Big City and how she liked working for a Jewish family.

The girl said everything was wonderful. She had her own room, her own television set, she had two days off each week, and they fed her well.

"But," she said, "They celebrate the funniest holidays!

"First they have a holiday that call 'Shabbos'*¹. That's when they eat in the dining room and they smoke in the bathroom.

"Then they have another holiday they call 'Tisha Bav.'*². That's when they smoke in the dining room and eat in the bathroom.

"But then they got another holiday which really is something! They call it 'Yom Kipper'*³. That's when they both eat and smoke in the bathroom!"

*¹—Sabbath.
*²—A day of fasting.
*³—Day of Atonement.

In the early Hitler days in Munich, a gang of Nazis rounded up the younger boys in pairs and instructed them to stand in front of Jewish stores to yell "Jew! Jew!"

Alfred Eichlerberg's tailor shop was one of those picked for this act of intimidation. The tailor was greatly distressed for, day after day, the young hoodlums stood in front of his shop.

"Jew! Jew!", they bellowed.

He didn't worry about his business falling off for he knew his faithful customers would still find a way to patronize him. But he felt humiliated. One day, he devised a plan. He approached the boys and said, "Any day you yell 'Jew' at me, I'll give each of you ten pfenning."

The boys were delighted!

The next day when they returned, Eichlerberg gave each of them only five pfenning. The boys complained but took the five pfenning for it was an easy way to make some money.

The next day when the boys came back all set to go about their jobs, Eichlerberg said, "I'm sorry, boys, but my business has fallen off so that I can no longer afford to pay you."

Angrily, one of the boys shouted, "First you gave us ten pfenning, then five, now you expect us to stand here and yell 'Jew' for nothing! Well, we'll get even with you! We're through!"

And they left.

A young rabbi, fresh from the seminary, was hired as a junior rabbi. He shared an office with a rabbi who had been with the synagogue for a great number of years. The two rabbis got along very well. But the younger rabbi was very curious about a ritual the elder rabbi observed every morning.

He arrived later than the younger man and after greeting his colleague, would open a little drawer in his desk with a key. Each morning, he took a card from the drawer, read it, replaced the card in the drawer and locked it with the key. He then put the key in another drawer.

The young rabbi was consumed with curiosity. It would have been a simple matter to take the key from the large drawer, open the smaller one, see what the elder rabbi read on the card each morning, and then replace the key. But he could not bring himself to do this. It seemed like a dishonest act to him.

After two years, the elder rabbi died and the younger rabbi was in charge of the synagogue. The office was now his alone. He went to the desk, found the key and removed the card and read, "Hebrew reads from right to left instead of left to right."

Little Brenda Orenstein came home from a friend's Christmas party. She was all excited about the tree and the bright, tinsley, twinkling ornaments.

"Mama, couldn't we have a Christmas tree too? Please, mommy . . . pretty please, mommy? I'll be the best little girl in the whole world if you say 'yes'!"

This presented quite a dilemma for Mrs. Orenstein. In the orthodox home in which she was brought up, a Christmas tree was equated much the same as the cholera. But the little girl continued to plead. She put her off by telling her she'd let her know tomorrow.

She went into her room and 'phoned the rabbi of the orthodox synagogue of which she was a member. She asked if he could sanction such a tree in her home.

"This is quite impossible! How could I possibly rationalize the use of such a tree in a Jewish home?"

Mrs. Orenstein persisted, "But maybe you could make a brucha* over the tree, which would put a different connotation on it."

"I am sorry but to me this would be a blasphemous act!"

Dejectedly, she hung up the receiver and 'phoned the rabbi of the conservative synagogue in the neighborhood. She asked the same favor of this rabbi and when he refused, suggested to him too that, perhaps, he could say a 'brucha' over it to make it acceptable.

"I'm sorry, Mrs. Orenstein, but I'm afraid that I could not possibly do as you ask. Jews do not celebrate Christmas!"

She decided to make one last try. She 'phoned the reform temple and asked this rabbi if he could possibly give her permission to put up a tree and suggested that he could make a 'brucha' over it.

"Why, of course you can put up a Christmas tree. You have my full permission to do so. Enjoy it!" and then he added, "Oh, by the way, Mrs. Orenstein, "What is a 'brucha'?"

Two members of the Israeli cabinet sat talking in a coffee house in Tel Aviv.

They were commiserating with each other about Israel's sad financial situation. Immigrants constantly pour in and there is barely enough money to care for them.

One of them said, "I think I have a solution! Why don't we declare war on the United States? You know what happens. The United States always wins! After the victory, she goes into the vanquished country, builds up industry, homes, roads; dredges the harbors; builds new airports and before you know it, the former enemy is a booming country!"

"Ah, my friend, my first thought is that your suggestion is a brilliant one. But with our hard luck, we're liable to win!"

---

*Brucha—*Hebrew for prayer.*

A wealthy American Jew retired and decided to settle in Israel Immediately, upon his arrival in Israel, he wrote the Prime Minister a letter. Since he planned on living the simple life in the Holy Land, he wanted to present the government with a check for three million dollars, practically his entire life's savings.

The Prime Minister was delighted and accepted the gift on behalf of his country. He said if there was anything he, the Prime Minister, could do, to call on him.

Mr. Dave Katz, the millionaire, did just that. He told the Prime Minister he had made his money in the wholesale meat business. And as a matter of fact, had started out as a chicken plucker. Before he died, he would be so happy if he had held some position of dignity. Could the Prime Minister possibly use him in the Cabinet?

The Prime Minister told him this was too momentous a decision to make on his own; he would have to consult with others in authority. As expected there was bedlam when the Knesset convened and at the Cabinet meeting as well.

His compatriots wanted to know what sort of intellectual or educational background did this man possess to equip him for so high a position? But in Israel, there is a saying that nothing is impossible; it just takes a little longer!

Mr. Katz was made Minister of Health and Welfare. And so today, his official duties require that he be at the pier as ships leave Israel. Through a large megaphone, he shouts to the departing tourists:

"FOOR GEZUNDTAHAIT."*

---

*Yiddish for "Travel in the best of health."

BLOOD IS THICKER THAN PRUNE JUICE

A bank in Israel advertised in the local paper. The ad read:

YOU MAY HAVE A FRIEND AT CHASE MANHATTAN BUT AT OUR BANK, YOU HAVE MESHPOCHEH!*

Hymie Warner had inherited a candy store from his father. The kids loved him and nick-named him "Hank." And he loved the kids . . . and also the candy.

He was getting on in years and sold his store . . . but he was bored. He decided to apply to Macy's for a job as Santa Claus. His twinkly blue eyes, quick smile and ample frame got him the job.

A few days before Christmas, the children were lined up to greet the big, fat, jolly Santa Claus in the toy department. The first little boy was patted on the back by Santa who boomed lustily, "Ho, ho, ho! What a nice little boy we have here! And what is your name, little man?"

"Patrick O'Connor."

"My, that's a fine name!" said Santa. "There's a big sack of toys and because you're such a nice little boy, you may take one!"

The second little child came up and Santa said, "Ho, ho, ho! What a pretty little girl we have here! And what is your name, little girl?"

"Mary Johnson."

"I can see you're a good little girl aside from a pretty one. Take a present from my big sack of toys!"

A third little boy came next.

"Ho, ho, ho!" bellowed Santa. "And what is your name, little boy?"

"Joey Rosenfeld."

"Ho, ho, ho!" said Santa, "And that's a fine name too!" and he whispered, "Take two!"

Yiddish for "relatives."

A famous dress designer, Mollie Charnes, was touring the Middle East looking for interesting and exotic ideas for fabrics and styling.

She landed in Egypt and the customs official started looking through her papers.

"We do not welcome Jews in the United Arab Republic! Are you a Jew?"

"Why, of course not! What ever made you think that?"

"Well, what is your religion?"

"Why, I'm a Seventh Avenue Adventist...what else?"

When Czar Alexander II was assassinated in 1881, his murder led to a surge of anti-Jewish pogroms throughout Eastern Europe. Between 1881 and 1905, some 550,000 Jews sought haven in the United States, many arriving in New York City.

Many of the immigrants were educated and trained in various crafts and professions. But many fields were closed to them, in some cases because of the language barrier and in others, because of discrimination. And so they flocked to the garment industries becoming operators, pattern-makers, pressers, designers, etc.

In one of these shops, a non-Jew was hired as a foreman. He turned out to be an anti-Semite. At every opportunity, he would go into the factory and make unkind remarks to humiliate the factory hands.

One of the pattern-makers, Sholom, was attending night school and was learning fast. One afternoon, the foreman came into the workroom and went into action. He bellowed about the "greenhorns" that were coming into this country which his ancestors had built up, and were trying to take over!

It was getting to be too much for Sholom.

"Just a minute, I learned in night school that a Jew named Haym Salomon gave this country a lot of his money to help finance the American Revolution against the British!"

"Yeah," said the foreman, "I know all about him. But I bet you can't name one other Jew that goes back to those days!"

"Just a minute," answered Sholom. "You heard of the Boston Tea Party? Well . . . who do you think was the caterer?"

After a "beatnik" poetry meeting, one of the bearded ones spoke to his friend.

"Hey, how come when I go to your house, your father gives me the fish-eye but your grandfather seems so friendly?"

"Oh, the old man thinks you're studying at the Yeshiva!"

An El Al plane was coming in for a landing in Tel Aviv. Over the loud-speaker, came the booming voice, "Pilot to tower, pilot to tower, flight 204 about to land, flight 204 about to land."

Seconds later, came another loud voice, "Tower to pilot, tower to pilot, do not land! We've just scrubbed the run-way and we haven't put down the newspapers as yet!"

Gamal Abdel Nasser decided to attend a Security Council meeting at the United Nations. One day he evaded his security guard and decided to see the sights of New York. He found himself down at the East River.

A young boy noticed him and followed him. Nasser leaned over the river's edge, the better to see his reflection in the water. He teetered on the edge and before he could save himself, he fell into the water. He yelled for help and the young boy jumped into the water and pulled him to safety.

"I owe my life to you" said Nasser. "What is your name?"

"My name is Israel Cohen, Mr. Nasser."

"Oh, you know who I am?"

"Yes sir."

"I'm very grateful to you. I'd like to repay you somehow. I'll give you anything you want or do anything you wish!"

"Please, Mr. Nasser," pleaded Israel, "I want just one thing...please don't tell my father!"

A teacher in a progressive school in the Sutton area announced she would call the roll. She asked that each child rise as his name was called and to express any thought that came to mind. She began:

"John Allen."

"I like to play with my electric trains."

"Michael Baker."

"I like summers 'cause then I can go to East Hampton."

"Donald Cohen."

"I pledge a thousand dollars."

Madison Avenue thinks up new gimmicks all the time. One of the newest is to have airplane stewardesses dressed in the native dress of the country which operates the airline instead of the regulation uniform.

And so on India airlines, the stewardesses now wear colorful saris; on Japanese planes, they wear kimonos; and so on.

And so on your next flight on El Al Airline, you will find matronly stewardesses wearing large aprons, saying to their passengers, "Eat, eat! Take a little nosh* !"

*Nosh—*Yiddish for nibbling between meals.*

This little story dates back to the days when the late Franklin D. Roosevelt was President.

One of the Manhattan chapters of B'nai B'rith was planning a function. A member of the board of trustees thought it would be a great idea to invite the President's mother, Sara Delano Roosevelt, as their guest of honor. The invitation was extended.

Mrs. Roosevelt replied that she would deem it an honor to attend, provided there was no admission charge for the function. She explained she did not want anyone to pay to see or hear her.

This presented a problem; catered dinners at fine hotels were costly. Sam Klein, of Union Square fame, was a member of this particular chapter. Someone came up with the bright idea that perhaps S. Klein would like to underwrite the cost of the affair. He was approached and agreed to do just that. He said he would if he could ask only one thing in return. He had recently brought his elderly mother over from Europe. If she could sit up on the dais with Sara Delano Roosevelt, he would consider it the happiest day of his life.

And so it was agreed.

The affair at the Waldorf was a brilliant one. On the dais, sat the handsome, stately Sara Delano Roosevelt. Next to her, Sam Klein sat beaming. His little, shriveled mother wearing a shaitel*[1] on her head sat on the other side of him.

After the dinner, Mrs. Roosevelt was introduced and said a few words of greeting. Everyone rose and applauded wildly. None was more jubilant than Sam Klein!

Still applauding, Mr. Klein turned to his mother and said, "A wonderful woman...the President's mother!"

Mrs. Klein nodded, "Yeh, yeh! Then she nudged her son and said, "Sam from what shule*[2] is her son the president?"

---

*[1]—Shaitel—*Jewish for wig worn by ultra-orthodox Jewish women.*
*[2]—Shule—*Jewish for synagogue.*

There was a notions convention scheduled in Madrid. Notions manufacturers from all over the world converged on the city. Eli Loew, one of the foremost American notions men, booked passage for Madrid.

He was tied up at the hotel and had just two days to go sight-seeing before returning home. He made a tour of the restaurants and night clubs and managed to get to a museum and a Flamenco dance festival.

While having dinner, a fellow conventioneer said, "What! You've been in Spain for over a week and you haven't even seen a bull-fight? Even if it means cancelling your plane reservation, you simply must go!"

Eli dashed over to the arena where the bull-fight was already in full swing. They had stopped selling tickets and he could hear the crowd roaring, "Ole! Ole!" He was determined to get inside but the gate was closed. He ran around to the side and noticed a door marked "Private" with a man standing guard there. He stood there trying to figure out how he could get in. Along came a bull-fighter who walked to the door and with a great flourish called out, "Toreador!" The guard opened the door saying "Entrar*1!" and he went through the door.

A few minutes later, another bull-fighter walked to the door, called out "Matador!" and again the guard opened the door and said, "Entrar!" A few minutes later, another came to the door, cried, "Picador!" The guard opened the door and again said, "Entrar!"

Eli came to a decision.

He walked over to the guard and with a great flourish, boomed, "Isadore!" The door opened and the guard said, "Kim arrine!*2"

An American visitor to Israel noticed an elderly Jew crying at the Wailing Wall, as if his heart were breaking. Overcome by such an outpouring, he approached the old man.

"My good man, may I help you? You seem to be crying bitter tears!"

"I want to be with my people!" groaned the old man.

"But you are with your people here... in the Promised Land!"

"No!... I want to be with my people... in Miami Beach!"

---

*1—*Spanish for "enter".*
*2—*Jewish for "enter".*

Many years ago, a group of us started an organization to fight bigotry and intolerance. Before long, we had a membership of several hundred people of all religions and races. We were an active group and ran many fund-raising functions.

We planned a luncheon and decided to feature a fashion show as part of the entertainment. An exclusive dress shop offered to supply the clothes if we would furnish our own models. I was one of the five women chosen by the committee. News photographers from the wire services photographed the models and then asked our names to be used in the captions.

There was a Goldstein, a Newberger, a Berger, a Cohen and I, a Blumenfeld! I quickly turned to my friend, Frances Cohen, who happened to be a Methodist, and suggested she use her maiden name. Inasmuch as we were not a Jewish organization, I thought the mention of only Jewish names would give that impression. She agreed and gave him her name as Frances Godby.

We watched for the pictures in the New York newspapers. None appeared! Somebody's grandmother was reading the Jewish Daily Forward and there, prominently displayed, was the picture of the five models. And Frances Godby's name appeared as Frances "Goldberg"!

A few years ago a tiny and talented young lady was hired as an editorial assistant on one of the leading national women's magazines. Her name was Sue Abramowitz.

The personnel director told her, very diplomatically, she had the qualifications they were looking for and she was hired. But he thought her name might be a little too long for the magazine's masthead. He suggested she change her last name.

Because she was so diminutive and had always been called "Little Sue" by her friends, she reversed the order and adopted "Sue Little" as her professional name. Her rise on the magazine was rapid. She became an associate editor and then editor-in-chief.

One day her secretary told her a young English girl had been hired as a researcher.

"And guess what her name is? None other than 'Sue Little'!"

"Take a memo, please," said the editor-in-chief gleefully, as she dictated:

"Miss Sue Little—Research Dept.

"I have just learned you have been hired as a researcher. I take this opportunity of welcoming you. You will note my name, too, is 'Sue Little'. This could lead to confusion. May I suggest you change your name? Perhaps a change to something like 'Sue Abramowitz' might be interesting."

> Cordially,
> Sue Little
> Editor-in-Chief

53

Mrs. Mintzer walked into Charles and Company, Ltd., ultra-fancy confectioners, The clerk, dressed in morning coat and striped trousers, asked, "May I help you madam?"

"Yes, you'll be so kindly, you'll give me a pound cookies what's in the window."

"I'll be glad to give you a pound of our Charles and Company petit fours. Would you care for anything else?"

"In the window, is also fancy shmancy candies. I'll take also a pound."

"Madam, at Charles and Company, these are called bonbons and I'll be happy to give you a pound of these as well. Will there be anything else?"

"Dot's all, denks!"

"And now where shall we deliver the petit fours and bonbons, madam?"

"Why deliver? What does it weigh? A little nothing!"

"But, madam, at Charles and Company, we are proud of our service and we would be glad to accommodate you if you so desire."

"It's very nice from you but it's a little bag and I only gotta carry it to the Bronx."

"But, madam," said the clerk. "Why shlepp*?"

*Carry—in *Yiddish.*

Many years ago, a Jew on a business trip to Shanghai was surprised but happy to learn that there was a synagogue in the city. On the Sabbath, he walked to the synagogue. On entering, he was amazed to find it filled with Chinese Jews with yellow complexion, prominent cheekbones, slanted eyes, short broad noses and straight black hair. They chanted the familiar Hebrew prayers. After services, many of the congregation flocked around him. Who was the stranger in their midst?

"I am a Jew from Chicago."

One of them said, "You are a Jew? You certainly don't look it!"

JUST KIDS

The family was up bright and early and mama was beside herself with joy! Today was her son's first day in school. She woke him with a kiss and said, "Bubbelle, mine darling, today you're a little man, you're starting school! And, Bubbelle dear, come you got to get dressed with your new suit. And you'll eat opp all your breakfast fast like mama's good little Bubbelle so you won't be late."

She walked him to school and left him with a goodbye kiss. "Now don't forget, Bubbelle, you shull be a good boy, mama shull be proud of her Bubbelle!"

She picked him up at noon, and said proudly, "Oy! I got such a big boy...going to school already. And tell me, Bubbelle, what did you learn today in your first day in school?"

"I learned my name is not Bubbelle, it's Oiving!"

A shiny, chauffeur-driven black Cadillac drove up to a hospital on the lower East Side of New York. A fashionably dressed woman got out and went inside, apparently to visit someone.

The driver found a parking space and again opened the door of the car and two tremendous black French Poodles waddled out. They were elegantly groomed and clipped and each wore a red leather collar encrusted with rhinestones.

The chauffeur, holding the two leashes, walked them to an empty lot down the street. Some of the neighborhood kids were playing baseball on the lot. When they saw the two animals, the game stopped. They had never seen anything quite like this before!

"Hey, mister!" asked one of the kids, "What the heck you got on the end of these leashes?"

"Dope!" answered his friend disgustedly, "Even if my father wasn't a furrier, I'd know! Can't you see... them's Persian Lambs!"

The Hebrew school teacher asked one of his students if he said his prayers before meals.

The proud little boy answered, "Oh, not me! I don't have to—my mom's a good cook!"

It was a miserable day and little Ruthie and Alfie were playing indoors. They played "Cowboys and Indians" for a while. Bored, Ruthie suggested that they play "house".

"Aw! That's a sissy game!"

"No," coaxed Ruthie, "It's fun. I'll be the mommy and you be the daddy. You must come home from the office and I'll make supper. After supper, we'll sit down and watch television. And then we must get in bed and talk Yiddish!"

"So what's new at your house?" a nosy neighbor asked of little Frankie Aronson.

"Who knows? They spell everything!" answered the little fellow.

A Texan and a New Yorker sat next to each other in an aeroplane flying to California.

A little boy sitting behind them began amusing himself by throwing little spit-balls into the Texan's ten-gallon hat. This infuriated the Texan and he bellowed, "You-all better stop that! If ah wuz your old man, I'd wring yo chicken-pickin' neck!"

Mr. Ginsberg was shocked! He said to the Texan, "What kind of a way is that to talk to a child? Talk nice. With honey, you get money!"

This made the Texan even madder. A few minutes later, Mr. Ginsberg left his seat and the Texan beckoned to the little boy. He offered him twenty-five cents if he would throw the spit-balls at Mr. Ginsberg when he returned. The deal was made.

Ginsberg sat down and started to read his magazine. The spit-balls whizzed by and at his head. Calmly, he turned to the little monster and said, "Little boy...do me a favor and go out and play!"

A little Catholic boy and a little Jewish boy were playing in the street.

All of a sudden the little Catholic boy said, "My priest knows more than your rabbi!"

"Why not...you tell him everything!"

The Bar Mitzvah boy was winding up his long speech before the assembled guests:

"And for making this Bar Mitzvah day possible, I should like to thank my dear parents, my beloved teacher, Mr. Cohen, and my psychiatrist, Dr. Freudinsky!"

The teacher asked Melvin, the son of a garment manufacturer, to name the four seasons.

Melvin thought a moment.

"Teacher, I can only think of two...busy and slack!"

The teacher was giving her class a geography lesson. She was asking for volunteers to tell which countries bordered other countries.

She noticed young Ezra doodling on a pad on his desk. He was obviously oblivious to what had been going on in the classroom. She asked Ezra to stand.

"Ezra, what do you know about the Roumanian border?"

Startled, Ezra blurted out, "Only that he goes out with my aunt and my father doesn't like it!"

There was big excitement in the Chanken home. Their little Stanley was starting Hebrew school that day.

Mama waited outside anxiously.

Stanley ran to mama beaming.

"Well, what did my little man learn on his first day?"

"I learned to write!"

"In one day you learned to write? What did you write?"

"How should I know?" answered Stanley. "I don't know how to read!"

A grandmother was wheeling a toddler in a stroller and holding the hand of another little boy.

She met an old friend she hadn't seen in years.

After the usual greetings, the woman said, "And these must be your grand-children! How old are they?"

The proud grandmother replied, "God bless them... the lawyer is two and the doctor is going on four!"

A little girl went to the grocery store for her mother. She asked for six rolls of bathroom tissue and asked the grocer to charge them. He remembered her face but, for the moment, couldn't remember her name.

"Darling, whom is this for?"

"Oh, we're all going to use it," answered the child.

One of the questions Miss Gollay asked of her fourth grade pupils was to name the Four Seasons. Little Velvel Greenblatt raised his hand and when called on answered, "Mustard, horseradish, garlic and vinegar."

A couple of enterprising Hasidic youngsters dressed up on Halloween, rang doorbells and called out, "Eppess for Yontiff?*"

*Yiddish for "something for the holiday".

Once upon a time, there was a little girl and her name was Little Red Rosenberg.

One day her mama told her that her grandma was not feeling so good and would she, like a sweet little doll, take a basket with some food to her poor, sick Grandma? Being a good little girl, she said she would.

Now the poor grandma who was sick, lived on the other side of the forest. Little Red Rosenberg, with basket slung over her arm, skipped off to bring her grandma some chopped liver, blintzes, gefilta fish,* chicken soup with matzoth balls and all kinds of goodies.

As she was skipping through the woods, the big bad wolf stopped her and asked where she was going with the basket of goodies. Naturally, being a friendly little girl, she told him. The big bad wolf next asked her where her grandma lived and she told him where and how to get there.

Of course, the big bad wolf ran on ahead, rushed into poor grandma's house, ate her up and got into her bed after putting on her nightgown and nightcap. He lay back smacking his lips as he contemplated eating Little Red Rosenberg when she arrived.

When Little Red Rosenberg walked into the bedroom and looked at what was supposed to be her nice grandma, she realized that something wasn't kosher. She said, "Grandma, what big ears you have!"

And the big bad wolf, in a falsetto voice murmured, "The better I should be hearing you with, mine dolling!"

"But Grandma, what big eyes you got!"

"The better to seeing you with, mine dolling!"

"But Grandma, what a big nose you have!"

Annoyed, the big bad wolf answered "Look who's talking!"

"Papa, I want to ask you a question" said little Julius after his first day in Sunday School.

"Yes, son, what is it?"

"The teacher was reading the Bible, about the Children of Israel building the temple, the Children of Israel crossing the Red Sea, the Children of Israel making sacrifices. Didn't the grown-ups do anything?"

A photographer, Harry Lederhandler, was walking around the lower East Side of New York City taking pictures of different typical characters and scenes.

He noticed an elderly, venerable looking gentleman, obviously a rabbi, walking with a little boy. They seemed very much engrossed in conversation.

After shooting his picture, he thought he'd walk by to eavesdrop on their conversation. Perhaps, he'd pick up a bit of Talmudic philosophy that he could use in his caption.

As he came closer, he heard the old man say, "Bummer! To a rabbi, you say 'bastard'?"

Jewish delicacies.

In a school on the lower East Side, the teacher, Mrs. Stern walked into the classroom and found the children sitting at attention in their seats.

Just as she was about to call the roll, she noticed a puddle on the floor near her desk.

"Who is responsible for this puddle?" she inquired.

No one answered.

'I would like the child responsible for the puddle to raise his or her hand."

Again silence...and no hand went up.

She removed a rag from one of her desk drawers and said, "I shall leave the room for a couple of minutes. I expect the child who is responsible for the puddle, to use this rag to wipe it up!"

She walked out of the room, closing the door behind her. She stayed out a few minutes, opened the door and looked for the puddle. Instead of one puddle, there were now two! She became quite angry and wasn't sure just how to proceed with the problem. She decided to walk slowly to her desk to give her a little more time to plan her next move. As she walked, she glanced up at the blackboard and there in large, bold letters in chalk, she read:

THE PHANTOM PISHER STRIKES AGAIN!

MISH-MASH

The 'phone rang and Rosie Cohen rushed to answer it.

A British voice, dripping with pomp and circumstance, said, "This is Mr. Clive Frothingham's secretary speaking. Mr. Frothingham regrets that he is unable to come for cocktails at seven."

"Oy, mister!" answered Rosie, "Have you got the wrong number!!!"

The Finebergs had saved for years for a trip around the world to celebrate their twenty-fifth wedding anniversary. They were particularly excited about going to the Orient. Friends and acquaintances volunteered advice.

"When you get to Hongkong" suggested a close friend, "Don't go to the tailor most Americans go to. Go to Wang Yee. He does a beautiful job on suits and is much more reasonable too." But unfortunately he didn't remember the exact location of the shop.

"Ask anyone in Hongkong. Everybody knows him and you'll thank me," assured his friend.

Mrs. Fineberg went shopping and her husband set out to find Wang Yee. He approached several Chinese but each motioned that he knew no English. He finally found one who understood and spoke English as well. He had never heard of a tailor named Wang Yee.

"But my friend was here just a few months ago" said Fineberg "and so there must be such a tailor."

"Have solution" said the Chinaman. "Over there is telephone booth. Simple! Look him up in the White Pages!"

There is a rumor of a merger of El Al and Alitalia Airlines which undoubtedly will be called "VAL-I'LL-TALIA".

In all planes, just before take-off and landing, a lighted sign flashes "FASTEN SEAT BELTS" and "NO SMOKING." On El Al planes, a third sign flashes "TAKE A PIECE OF FRUIT"!

Milton Kramer was stationed in Peachtree, Georgia, during the second World War. One day, he 'phoned mama in New York. He was excited! He was in love! He was getting married the next day and he wanted mama to be the first to know!

With trepidation, mama said, "Miltie, mine dear, I hope she's a Jewish girl!"

Milton spurted out, without catching his breath, that he'd gone to the canteen expecting to be bored and there was this beautiful Georgia peach and it turned out that she was Jewish!

Mama was relieved and happy and with choked voice, gave her blessing. She had only one thing to ask, that they be married by a rabbi.

"But, Mom, there are practically no Jews in this town and they don't have a rabbi!"

"So I'll send you down one. So you'll wait a couple days, just for mama."

Milton consented.

Mama went right down to Rivington Street and made arrangements with the chief rabbi of Rivington Street, no less! He was delighted to go! He had seen only Minsk, Brooklyn and New York City in his sixty-odd years. This was a big occasion for him. He took out his Saturday best, new black trousers topped by his long black, silk coat, his large beaver bowler hat and his black silk umbrella. He carefully brushed his beard and side-curls which hung just below his ears and he was off.

When he landed in Peachtree, he walked slowly looking for the address mama had written on a piece of paper. As he walked, he was suddenly conscious of someone back of him. He turned and saw there were a few people who seemed to be following him. He decided he must be wrong. Thank God, in America anyone could walk where he wished! If he could walk down Main Street so could they! So with paper in hand, he continued to walk and look for the house.

Confusion seemed to be mounting behind him. He turned again. Instead of the few people he had seen a few minutes before, the whole town seemed to be following him. He straightened himself up to his full five feet, turned around once more and stammered, "What's amatter? You never seen maybe before a Yenkee?"

A "Briss"*—is a surgical function worked into a catered affair.

*Briss—*A circumcision ceremony.*

61

They had just buried Alex Klinger and his relatives and friends stood sadly by as the rabbi said the final prayers at the grave. The rabbi turned to one of the mourners and asked his name and relationship.

"My name is Morris Shein and I was a partner of the deceased."

The rabbi chanted the Kaddish* in Hebrew and ended the prayer wtih the name "Morris Shein".

He turned to another man and asked his name and relationship.

"My name is Ben Wolkoff and I was his star salesman."

Again, the rabbi chanted mournfully in Hebrew ending the prayer with the name "Ben Wolkoff."

The rabbi addressed a man standing a bit back from the mourners with the same question.

"I'm an old friend, Meyer Rappaport, and I'm a talent scout."

The rabbi said, "A talent scout?" and in a booming voice sang out, "Some enchanted evening!"

Isadore Lapidus was a dress salesman who went on the road several times a year.

One day, he stopped his car on the main street of a small town. He had been driving for hours and was parched. He noticed a general store which sold drugs, hardware, farm supplies and had a soda fountain.

He walked in and the proprietor said, "What can I do for you, young man?"

"You handle maybe fertilizer?"

"I sure do!"

"Alright, so wash your hands and make me a vanilla malted!"

A martian landed on Broadway right in front of Lindy's Restaurant. The window featured a display of bagels. The martian was baffled. He walked into the restaurant and inquired of the cashier.

"What do you do with those wheels that you have in the window?"

"Those are not wheels," replied the cashier, "They're bagels!"

"Bagels, huh?" said the martian, "I bet they'd go nicely with lox!"

One of the operators in a dress factory asked her fellow worker if she could recommend a doctor.

"Oy, have I got a doctor? His name is Dr. Abner Sternfeld. He's a living doll! He's so good that if you can't afford an operation, he'll even touch up your X-rays!"

---

*Kaddish—*a prayer for the dead.*

Mrs. Blumberg was reading a story on India in the Jewish Daily Forward. She turned to her husband.

"Max, what's an 'untouchable'?"

"A guy you can't borrow money from!"

Kalman Katzenellenbogen had lived a hard life. He had lost his small business selling twine in the garment district. He was all alone in the world. He now operated a small soda fountain-candy store on the East Side. The store was so small, he could squeeze no more than the name "Katzen" on the awing. Empty soda bottles returned by customers crowded the already cramped quarters. More often than not, the bottles were turned in dirty.

One day, he received an odd-shaped, dirtyish brown bottle. He took a rag and started rubbing off some of the dirt from the bottle. And out of the bottle came a genie ...but this was a Jewish genie! The genie told old man Katzenellenbogen he was prepared to grant three wishes to anyone who asked them.

Kalman said, "I'm an old man. For the last ten years, I haven't bought a suit but who needs it? I wear an apron day and night and sleep in the back of the store. So I wish I was young again and wearing an outfit I should look like a real sport!"

"Poof"... went the genie and there was Kalman young again and dressed in natty sports clothes!

Kalman said, "Oy! Could I use a vacation but who'll mind the store?"

The genie said he would.

Katzenellenbogen said, "I wish I was at Grossinger's having a good time with the young girls again!"

"Poof"... blew the genie and Kalman was transported to Grossinger's.

Then one of the regular customers arrived at the store.

"Where is Mr. Katzen?"

The genie explained the owner had gone away for a vacation and he was running the business.

"Awright, then" she said, "I wish you'd make me a malted!"

So the genie went "Poof" and she became a malted.

As I was walking along Rivington Street in New York City I saw a retail store with the sign "Rabinowitz and O'Brien."

I was greeted inside by a small man with a beard and wearing the traditional skull cap.

I said "It's good news to me to see how the Jews and the Irish have become such good friends and have even become business partners."

"I got more news for you," he said, "I'm O'Brien."

A "K-nocker"* is a guy who works crossword puzzles with a fountain pen.

Mrs. Cohen was waiting for a bus and all of a sudden she heard a loud scream, "Well, if it ain't my old friend, Franny Cohen!" They embraced and Franny said, "It must be fifteen years since we gave out milk together in school for the P.T.A.!"

"Franny, you haven't changed a day! You still look like a spring chicken! But tell me about your sons. You had a son, Abie. How is Abie?"

"Please...Abie is no more Abie! Abie is now Abercrombie! He became a doctor! You should see his office. Rockefeller couldn't have a nicer one! His patients are all from the four hundred. For tonsils, without adenoids, he takes $300! I'm telling you, all my good friends should do so well."

"That's wonderful! And how is your son, Benny?"

"Please...Benny is no more Benny! Benny is now Byron! And is he a lawyer! Louis Nizer takes lessons from him! He wouldn't even take an accident case; only million dollar cases he takes. I'm telling you...he's making a fortune!"

"You had also a third son, Izzy. So how is Izzy?"

"Well," said Franny," Izzy was Izzy and he's still Izzy. He was a pants presser and he's still a pants presser! And believe me, if it wasn't for Izzy, we'd all die from hunger!"

In the showroom of Schwartz and Weiss, buyers were looking over the mink coats on the rack, and placing their orders.

Finally, the showroom was empty except for one buyer and the two partners.

The buyer turned to Schwartz and said, "Irving, I heard you moved to the suburbs. How do you like living there?"

"Well, to tell you the truth, at first it didn't appeal to me. But now, that I got myself a paramour, believe me, I would recommend it to all my friends!"

The buyer looked a little shocked, signed the order and left.

Weiss flew into a rage!

"Dope, what kind talk is this? If you're fooling around with one of the models, does the whole damn world gotta know, including the buyers?"

Annoyed, Schwartz came back. "What are you crazy or something? Who's talking about models? You know when I first moved to the house, every time I mowed mine lawn with the hand-mower, mine back was killing me! Since I bought mine paramour, everything is hunky-dory!"

---

*K-nocker—*Jewish for a wise-guy.*

A Jewish insurance agent, just starting on a job was given a prospect, the president of a large company. Several agents had been trying to sell him a policy without success. He was told that if he was able to write the policy, to expedite matters, it would be advisable to bring back a specimen of the man's urine.

Elated, the agent returned several hours later with the policy in one hand and a large pail in the other.

His boss was pleased.

"But what have you got in the pail?"

"What do you mean 'what'? I followed your instructions. I sold the company a group policy!"

Leo Epstein was drafted and stationed at Fort Dix for basic training. Never had Uncle Sam a more inept recruit to deal with! He just couldn't seem to do the simplest things right. If his commanding officer said, "Forward march", he retreated; "at ease", he'd march. He wound up doing KP more than he trained. He was a constant source of irritation to the officers and the laughing stock of the base.

A directive came through for fifty men to be shipped overseas for immediate combat. The colonel put his name on the top of the list, delighted to be rid of him.

The men were thrown immediately into the Battle of the Bulge. Newspapers began to carry bold headlines of the daring young hero of the Battle of the Bulge, none other than one, Leo Epstein! "Leo Epstein single-handedly captures a hundred Germans!" "Epstein wipes out machine-gun nest!"

Our hero went on to braver and bolder exploits. At the end of the war, he was awarded the Congressional Medal of Honor. And his chest was covered with numerous other medals and ribbons.

His former buddies and officers were flabbergasted. They couldn't understand how this dud could turn into this great hero!

When the fighting ended in Europe, the Fort Dix officer ran into Leo's European officer and, naturally, our hero became the topic of their conversation.

"Tell me," said his former colonel, "What happened that this shlemiel who couldn't follow a single order turned into a big hero?"

"Very simple! I handed him a gun and ammunition and said to him: Epstein, take this and remember, you're in business for yourself!"

A psychiatrist and a proctologist decided to merge their offices to cut down on expenses.

To further economize, they had one sign printed:

Dr. Eli Wolf, Psychiatrist
Dr. Morris Fink, Proctologist
Specializing in Odds and Ends.

Liebowitz, the tailor, retired and moved to the country to live with a married daughter and her family. It was a charming house, the countryside was beautiful and he was made to feel welcome. But the peace and quiet after thirty years in New York City began to get on his nerves. One day, he went for a long walk and came upon a convent about two miles down the road. As he approached, one of the nuns came out of the gate and greeted him. He returned the greeting and they got into a conversation.

Liebowitz told her he was a retired tailor and was now living with his daughter down the road.

"By the way, Sister, do you need maybe a good tailor by you in the convent? I'll work cheap. Money, I don't need! I need a little part-time job, it should occupy my time."

She told him she'd inquire of the Mother Superior and let him know. And so Liebowitz went to work at the convent, every afternoon but Saturday. He seemed a happy man once more.

After working there a few weeks, his friend, Sister Margaret, came in to visit him After inquiring about his health, she said, "Mr. Liebowitz, you're a fine craftsman and the Mother Superior is very content with your work. Only I have a favor to ask of you. When you speak to the Mother Superior, please try to remember, it's 'Mother Superior' not 'Mother Shapiro'."

Two old cronies were walking home from a lodge meeting.

"So what is your son doing for a living?" asked one.

"He got some crazy idea in college and studied to be a psychologist."

"So how is he doing?"

"Not bad!"

"Why not?" answered his friend. "I understand these fellers pick up plenty of change that falls behind the couch!"

A man walked into a kosher restaurant. He sat down and was approached by a Chinese waiter who asked for his order in Yiddish. He told the waiter what to bring him, ate his dinner and took the check to the register to pay it.

The proprietor was the cashier. As the customer was paying his check, the proprietor asked if he had enjoyed his dinner.

"Yes," answered the customer. "Everything was fine. One thing surprised me though. I never met a Chinaman who talks Yiddish before!"

"Shhhhhh!" admonished the proprietor. "Not so loud! He thinks we're teaching him English!"

A young woman and an older woman, both ardent workers in the Ladies Auxiliary, became quite friendly.

One day, over lunch, the young woman asked her companion, "Darling, I'd like to ask a confidential question of you. How does one go about starting an affair?"

"Always the same way, my dear," answered the older woman, "First, with the singing of The Star Spangled Banner and then Hatikvah!"*

On a plane headed for Hawaii, two friends got into a discussion about the pronunciation of the word "Hawaii". One said the "w" was pronounced as a "v"; the other argued that the word was pronounced as it is spelled. They decided to ask a native when they landed.

At the airport, the passengers were greeted with music, and friendly natives bedecked them with flowers and leis. The two friends pumped the hand of a particularly friendly native.

"Tell me, my good man," asked the tourist, "Do you pronounce your island 'Hawaii' or 'Havaii'?"

"Havaii," came the quick reply.

"Thank you very much," said the American.

"You're velcome!"

In one of the suburbs in Westchester, a Jewish Center has just been completed.

It is so ornate and so expensive, they named it OUR LADY OF PERPETUAL SIMCHAS*.

Later money was appropriated for an additional wing in which they will build a split-level succah*.

---

*The Jewish national anthem.
*Simchas—joyous occasions.
*Succah—a special room used for a Jewish holiday.

67

NOODNICKS AND SHNOOKS

Mrs. Kantor, with five children aged thirteen to twenty-two, was feeling poorly. And she seemed to be putting on weight. She visited her gynecologist. She surmised that she had a tumor. After the examination, the doctor informed her that she had no tumor but that she was pregnant.

"Oh, no!" shrieked Mrs. Kantor.

"Now, now, don't take it that badly, Mrs. Kantor. You're still a young woman!" consoled the doctor. "And your children are of an age where they can be of considerable help to you. So, just console yourself!"

"It's not that, Doctor! I just can't bear the thought of having to attend another P.T.A. meeting!"

Two partners, Mort and Harry, enjoyed a congenial relationship. Mort was married; Harry, a bachelor. After hours one day, over a bottle of scotch, they began to exchange confidences.

"How come you never married, Harry? I know you go out on dates all the time."

"It's a long, sad story but since you asked, I'll tell you. I was in love several times but each time I was discouraged from marrying. The first girl I wanted to marry, I thought was perfect. She was intelligent and beautiful and came from a good family. I brought her home to meet my parents. My mother didn't like her looks so I broke it up. Then I met another girl at the Laurels up in the Mountains. I thought she was the type my mother would really approve of. I brought her home. My mother liked her looks but she didn't like the way she talked. There were a few more girls and each time, my mother found some fault and each time that ended the romance. Last year, I went skiing. I met a girl who was so like my mother, she even looked like her. She dressed with the same flair as my mother, talked like her, had the same tastes and everything. I felt my mother would certainly like her!"

"Well, didn't she?" inquired Mort.

"Yeah, she did! But my father hated her!"

One of the ladies of the Sisterhood was talking excitedly about her wonderful trip to Israel.

"Did you go by chartered flight?" asked her friend.

"No."

"By group flight?"

"No."

"Did you have an excursion rate?"

The answer again was "no."

With surprise in her voice, her friend said, "You mean you traveled retail?"

A man telephoned the Israel Bond Office and said he would like to speak to someone about some bonds he bought some years ago.

The operator asked: "Are you interested in conversion or redemption?"

The caller paused, then inquired: "Say, is this Israel Bonds or the Christian Mission?"

A Jewish taxi driver picked up two women and was driving them to their destination. One of them lit a cigarette and called to the driver:

"You don't have an ashtray back here and I'd like to flick the ashes from my cigarette."

"Lady," answered the driver, "Just flick them on the floor. I got a woman coming in three times a week!"

Two old friends, one a bachelor and the other married, met after a lapse of many years.

The bachelor asked about his friend's health. "I'm fine, thank God!"

"And how is your wife?"

"Yes and no...but thank God, right now, yes."

"And your children...tell me about your children!"

"My two girls are married and I have three grandchildren, they should live and be well, like dolls! And my boy is at Columbia, an A number one student and such an athlete yet too!"

"Well" said the bachelor, "It was so nice to see you and I hope we'll meet again sometime soon." And he started to walk away.

The married one called after him.

"What kind of friend are you? We haven't seen each other in years. You ask about my health, my wife's and inquire about my children. Aren't you interested in how I'm doing financially? How come you didn't ask me about my business?"

"All right," said the bachelor, "You want I should ask about your business, I'll ask! How's business?"

"Oy!" wailed his friend, "Don't ask!"

Sam Mandelbaum sat sadly through funeral services in a chapel for an old friend. When all the mourners had left, he approached the custodian of the chapel and said he would like to place an order for a casket for himself, to be held in readiness for him when his time came. He showed him a casket that cost a thousand dollars.

"It's not bad but I'd like to see a little nicer one."

He was shown one for fifteen hundred dollars.

"It's a little better...but it looks like it might go through at the elbows."

The man showed him one for two thousand dollars.

This was a little more like what he wanted but he said, "For a man of mine means, instead of the dark wood, it should be maybe pickled pine. Instead of wooden handles, I'd like better silver ones. And instead of the regular lining, I'd like better a good quality skinner satin."

He was told that this would be a custom job and would cost him five thousand dollars.

Mandelbaum signed the order, made out a check and went back to his shop. His partner greeted him, they had a drink and talked philosophically about the uncertainties of life.

"Yes," said Sam, "Who knows when his number is up next? It shouldn't happen to a dog. But, God forbid it should happen, at least I know I'll be laid to rest in a decent box."

Sam told his partner that he had ordered a casket for himself.

"How much did it set you back?"

"It ain't cheap but wait till you see it. It's a beauty! It cost me five thousand dollars!"

"Five thousand dollars!" cried his partner. "Dope, for another few hundred dollars, you could be buried in a Cadillac!"

The meeting of the ladies' auxiliary broke up and Lenore and Adele walked down 72nd Street together since they both lived on West End Avenue.

Lenore said, "You know, Delly, the speaker of the afternoon is absolutely right. We women should really take a greater interest in world affairs. By the way, what do you think of the Common Market?"

"That's not for me, kiddo," answered Adele. "I still prefer to deal at Gristede's!"

A fellow ran up to another man, slapped him on the back and said, "Hello Goldberg! How are you?"

He who got slapped, in an annoyed tone said, "My name isn't Goldberg! And what's the idea of slapping me so hard on the back?"

"It's your business what I do to Goldberg?"

A "shnook"*—is a co-signer with a fountain pen.

---

*Schnook—*Yiddish for an easy-going gullible fellow.*

While on a safari in darkest Africa, Sam Spiegel was startled to hear someone call out, "Hello Sam! What are you doing here?"

Sam asked, "Who are you? And how do you know my name?"

The man answered, "Don't you remember me? I'm Jake Fineberg and I used to sell you zippers and linings on Seventh Avenue."

"Yes, now I remember you, Jake. But what are you doing here in this part of the world?"

"Well," replied Jake, "I got tired of the rat-race and came here to live. But what are *you* doing here?"

"It's like this," said Sam, "I retired from the business and I was bored and unhappy. I went to a psychiatrist and he suggested I take up a hobby. I tried painting, stamp-collecting, ceramics but nothing kept my interest. Then my psychiatrist suggested collecting unusual insects. So I decided on a safari. So here I am and, as yet, I haven't even found an interesting specimen!"

Just then an insect lit on Jake's arm. He caught it and handed it to Sam.

"How's this?"

"Just fair."

Jake picked one off a dog lying on the ground.

"Here's a beaut, Sam!"

Sam was not impressed. Jake gathered up a few more running about. Nothing pleased his old customer.

"Well," said Jake, "I'm sorry I can't satisfy you. But thanks for looking at my line, anyway!"

A friend of mine, a TV executive, lives in Larchmont. His neighbor's daughter was to participate in a Westchester Catholic Cotillion to be held at the Plaza.

My friend mentioned the invitation to one of his confreres at the station. He said that he would probably be the only Jew at the party and added that the Cardinal would also be present.

"In that case," remarked his colleague, "You'll probably have to kneel and kiss the Cardinal's ring."

"Who's kissing?" was the rejoinder. "I'm appraising!"

A little old lady walked into a kosher butcher shop and asked for a beautiful four pound chicken. The butcher showed her several which she quickly rejected. The butcher went back into the large refrigerator and produced one he called a real prize.

She was not quite convinced. She started to feel every part of the chicken, inspecting the legs, wings and neck. The butcher was getting annoyed.

"Lady," he finally said, "Tell me one thing! Do you think you could pass such a test?"

There was a lecture at the Golden Age Club and the hall was filled to capacity. When the lecture ended, the members sat around chatting and partaking of refreshments.

Mr. Saxe, aged seventy-six, approached a pretty white-haired member.

"How would you like to have a date with a Sugar Daddy Saturday night?"

"I'd like that fine!"

"So, all right, I'll pick you up at eight!"

Dressed in her Saturday best, she awaited her date. He arrived on time. She was disappointed when he suggested they go to the neighborhood movie which was cut-rate to members of the Golden Age Club. She was sure that he would make up for it by taking her to an elegant eating place after the movie. Instead, they wound up for coffee in a cafeteria next to the movie.

Wounded, she blurted out: "I thought you said you were a 'Sugar Daddy'?"

Undaunted, Saxe replied: "But I am! For twelve years already, I got diabetes!"

Two Martians landed on earth and ran into each other.

"Hi!" said the first Martian, "What's your name?"

"428,629,382! And what's yours?"

"Mine's 664,935,715."

"That's funny," said the first! "You don't look Jewish!"

The Rabbi announced his sermon would deal with Moses. At the mention of the name "Moses," the Rabbi thought he heard a voice from the rear of the synagogue shout "shmo!" He figured he must be wrong and continued.

He spoke of Moses, the great spiritual leader who led the children of Israel out of bondage. Again, at the mention of "Moses," he heard the same voice call out "jerk!" He continued, telling how Moses asked God to send manna from the Heavens to feed the children of Israel.

Each time Moses' name was mentioned, he heard the same angry muttering. The Rabbi related how Moses prayed, the Red Sea parted and the children of Israel were permitted to cross into freedom.

Again, came an even louder "Shmo!" The Rabbi could contain himself no longer.

"Why are you mad at Moses?"

"Why shouldn't I be mad? When Moses crossed over the Red Sea, if he had turned left instead of right, the Arabs would have had the sand and we would have had the oil!"

The whole mah jongg group was invited to the home of a new member who had just joined the group.

Someone admired a lamp. The hostess volunteered, "Yes, I got it with Octogan soap coupons."

Another one of the girls admired a painting on the wall.

"Yes, I got that too with Octogan soap coupons."

A piano was the next object singled out for praise.

"Isn't it a beauty? I got that with Octogan soap coupons too."

As the girls walked around, everything that was admired had been obtained with the soap coupons.

One of the players noticed that one room was locked. "Your home and everything in it is just gorgeous. But what's in the room with the door closed?"

"Octogan soap, what else!"

Ulcers had plagued Hymie Feldbaum for years. But his family could not get him to change his eating habits. He became very ill and was finally hospitalized and fed intravenously.

As soon as his strength was restored, loud cries were heard coming from his room. Dr. Tirsch was summoned and Hymie began to complain. "Please, doctor, my arm is stiff like a board already! You gotta do something! A person can stand so much and no more!"

The doctor comforted him by saying that he would stop the intravenous feeding and leave orders that he be fed instead through a rectal tube. Feldbaum protested, "Who could live only on sugar and water? Maybe they could give me better a little pickled herring and maybe a little tea with lemon?"

"Look, Mr. Feldbaum, I'm trying to get you well so don't ask the impossible of me!"

"Doctor, I give you my word, if you don't change mine diet, I'll take my business elsewhere!"

The doctor, just to placate him, said that he'd leave instructions with the nurse to give him tea with lemon instead of the glucose.

Later on, the nurse came in, inserted the rectal tube and left. Loud screams of "Gevalt" and "Aye, aye, aye" brought the nurse rushing to his room.

"What's the matter, Mr. Feldbaum, too hot?"

"Who's complaining too hot? It's too sour!"

A presser in a tailor shop arrived one morning wearing a good sized diamond ring. One of the tailors noticed the sparkler and asked about it.

"My mother-in-law gave me a thousand dollars before she passed away. She said that when she dies, I should buy a beautiful stone. So I did!"

An elderly Jew was crossing the street. A car turned the corner at high speed and knocked the old man down. A crowd gathered as the man lay there apparently unconscious.

Someone ran for a priest. The good Father rushed to the old man and started to administer last rites. He began to chant, "Do you believe in the Father, the Son and the Holy Ghost?"

The old man suddenly opened his eyes and whined, "I'm dying and he's asking me riddles!"

An elderly Jewish lady walked into an appetizing store and said she wanted a nice shmaltz herring. The man dipped into the barrel and came up with a fine-looking fat herring. The old lady didn't like its looks. He dipped in again and again and each time, she found fault with his choice. He dug way down to the bottom of the barrel and picked out a real prize. That one suited her.

"How much for the herring?"

"Twenty-nine cents."

"Twenty-nine cents for such a little herring! Across the street, the same herring is twenty-one cents!"

"So buy it across the street!"

"I can't," explained the old lady, " 'Cause they're all out of herrings!"

Exasperated, the dealer retored:

"Look, lady, when I'm out of them, I charge twenty-one cents also!"

On the way home from a Sisterhood meeting, Fanny said to her companion, "Tell me, Bessie, what do you think of Red China?" "Please, Fanny," retorted Bessie in a tone of utter disgust, "Not with your yellow tablecloths!"

The weekly canasta game resumed after the summer. One of the players had just returned from Europe and her friends were eager to hear about her experiences.

"Were you in Rome?"

"Of course!"

"What did you think of the Colosseum?"

"It's nice...if you like 'modern'!"

A little old Jewish lady went to a gynecologist. After asking her the preliminary questions, the doctor said, "Please go into the next room and take off all your clothes."

"All my clothes?" said the surprised little lady.

"Yes, all your clothes."

"Oy, does your mama know what you're doing for a living?"

There once were two brothers, Max and Yonkel. Max never went near the synagogue. Yonkel was the pious one. To him, the synagogue was more like a second home.

One day Yonkel went to the synagogue with a heavy heart. He cried out in anguish:

"Oh Lord, all my life I have been like a devoted son to you! Every day, I come to the synagogue and pray. And I am a charitable man. Never have I made a decision in my whole life without first coming here to pray to you. Before I chose a bride, I consulted with you; before I make a business deal, I come and pray and consult with you. And I am a poor man! I never know where my next piece of bread is coming from. And my brother, Max... he never comes near the synagogue. He spends his time instead at the race track and thinks only of the gay life yet he is a rich man! Oh, God! Why have you punished me like this? What have I done to you to deserve this?"

There was a loud noise which seemed to come from the Heavens and Yonkel heard:

" 'Cause you're all the time noodging me!"

When Samson Levine arrived in New York from Poland, there were no child-labor laws. And so, at the age of eight, he was out on the streets peddling shoe-laces. He never went to school.

When he was a little older, he worked running errands and sweeping up in a dry-goods store on Orchard Street. He then began to wait on the customers. Before too many years, he became a junior partner. The store grew and so did Samson's bankroll.

When the time came for him to open an account in the bank, he could not sign his name. He had learned to write figures and he used two X's as his signature at the bank. He continued to add to his account until it became a sizeable one.

One day, the senior partner died and Samson was the sole owner of the store. He also bought the building in which the store was housed, as well as several of the adjoining buildings.

He went to the bank one Friday, as had been his custom for years, to make a deposit. But this time, he asked to see the manager. He was shown to his desk.

"Good afternoon, Mr. Levine. What can I do for you?"

"Well, you see it's like this. I'd like you to change your records on my account. I want from now on, my signature should be three X's instead of two!"

"We can do that for you if you wish it." His curiosity got the better of him, "But why?"

"Well... my wife feels that a man in my financial position, should have a middle name!"

The old Jewish man was on the witness stand and the prosecuting attorney asked him how old he was.

"I'm *kenahorrah, seventy-three years old."

The prosecuting attorney said:

"Please just answer the question, nothing else. How old are you?"

"I'm kenahorrah, seventy-three years old."

The prosecuting attorney was losing patience. The judge intervened. He suggested the old man answer the attorney's question, and only the question, or be held in contempt of court.

The defense attorney came forward and asked the judge if he might ask the question of the witness. The judge agreed. The defense attorney turned to the old man and said:

"Kenahorrah, how old are you?"

The old man answered:

"Seventy-three years old."

One day while relaxing on the beach, a friend asked Becky Shmulowitz how come she named her son "Stetson."

"It always bothered me, Becky. What kind of name is that for a Jewish boy?"

"Well, you see it's like this: For ten years I was married and it looked like I would never have a baby. Naturally, Jake and I were very unhappy about it. Thank God, at last, I became pregnant! My whole family and all our friends were so excited! And everybody was giving us suggestions to name the baby. We didn't want to hurt anyone's feelings. When at last we were blessed with a son, everyone came to the 'briss' and again, they all started with the names. My husband had a solution. He took someone's hat, gave each one a piece of paper and told them to write down names, and then to put them in the hat. Then he asked me to pick out a name. I shuffled the names good. One name got stuck. I figured that must be the one! I gave a good pull and out came 'Stetson'!"

It was Armed Services Day and Fifth Avenue was crowded with spectators watching the parade. The day was unbearably hot. An elderly Jew fainted and dropped to the pavement.

People around him became excited. Someone shouted, "Give him air! Don't crowd around him!" Someone else shouted, "Someone run and get him some water!"

The old man opened his eyes and wailed weakly, "Please, if you'll be so kindly, make it a malted instead!"

Mrs. Portnoff was stopped by a pan-handler.

"You know, lady, I haven't eaten in three days!"

"That's terrible! So you should force yourself!"

---

*Kenahorrah—A Yiddish expression used by superstitious Jews to ward off the evil eye.

The ladies were playing gin rummy at the home of one of the members of the Sisterhood. Rebecca was leaving and told her hostess she had enjoyed her hospitality.

"And your home-made cookies were so delicious that, believe it or not, I ate four!"

"You ate six—but who's counting?"

Bernard Gimbel walked around the main floor of Gimbel's one morning. Those who recognized him, greeted him. Hymie Lapidus noticed and said, "Good morning. You must be Mr. Gimbel."

Mr. Gimbel replied he was and asked if there was anything he could do for him. Lapidus said he had recently sold his own store, was looking for a new business and asked Mr. Gimbel if he'd be interested in selling his store.

Gimbel replied he would sell if the price was right, figuring the gentleman was pulling his leg.

"How much you're asking?"

Mr. Gimbel thought he'd play along and said, "Well, not less than seventy-five million."

"Mr. Gimbel, I want you should know I never buy a proposition before my wife, Becky, don't look at it too."

He assured Mr. Gimbel he would be back in the morning with his wife and asked where he could find him. Gimbel told Lapidus he'd be at the same place at 11 o'clock the next morning.

The next morning, bright and early, Lapidus arrived with his wife. They both walked up and down each aisle inspecting the merchandise. Gimbel could hardly believe it but at eleven, the two of them approached him.

"Well?" he asked, "Have you come to any decision?"

Lapidus replied, "My wife, Becky, and I have been looking around. You got beautiful merchandise; a nice location, near Macy's; and the price ain't bad! But my wife found it has one big fault...no rooms in the back to live!"

A haughty-looking Englishman and his equally haughty-looking wife sat at a table in Lindy's. They were ignored by the waiter who was busy advising and taking orders from his regular customers.

Finally they were able to catch the attention of the waiter, who came to their table—and belched.

"Sir," said the Englishman. "You belched before my wife."

"Wottsamattah, it was her turn first?"

Jake wept at his wife's funeral. But Moe, their boarder, was completely broken up and cried hysterically.

Jake consoled him. "Moe, don't take it so hard. I'll get married soon again."

Morris was flying down to Miami to visit a daughter. The man in the next seat began to talk to him. He was obviously a man of considerable means and spoke of his boat and his golf club. Morris, not to be outdone, said that he too belongs to a golf club and plays very often now that he's retired.

"If you play often, you're probably a good golfer."

"Very good, if I must say so myself!"

"Do you play in the low 70's?"

"Of course!" retorted Morris. "But when it's colder than that, I quit!"

Two old friends ran into each other on the boardwalk at Atlantic City.

"Why darling, you look marvelous! What are you doing with yourself?"

"I must confess...I'm having an affair!"

"Congratulations, darling! Who's the caterer?"

An elderly Jewish gentleman happened to witness an automobile accident. He was called as a witness for the plaintiff at the trial for damages.

The prosecutor asked him, "Did you see the accident in question?"

"How could I not see it? Wasn't I there?"

"Were you walking in the street at the time?"

"What then, I was maybe flying?"

"Would you say that the defendant was at fault?"

"Who then, I was at fault, maybe?"

The judge, obviously annoyed, interrupted the cross-examination and said to the witness, "Why do you answer every question with another question?"

"So, why not?"

According to statistics, in eighteen percent of American homes, the wives handle the money and keep the records.

In one such home in Rockaway, the wife was sitting at her desk balancing the family checkbook. Her husband reclined in his favorite chair reading the evening newspaper.

He looked up from his newspaper and said, "By the way, Debby, what do you think we ought to do about the Taft-Hartley bill?"

"I'll check it and, if we owe it, I'll pay it!"

A man was eating his dinner in Moskowitz and Berkowitz's Famous Restaurant on Allen Street.

A typical, flat-footed Jewish waiter passed his table carrying a tray loaded with food.

"I beg your pardon, waiter," said the man, "but would you be good enough to tell me what time it is?"

"This ain't my table!"

A man walked up to another and said, "Walberg! What happend to you? You used to be short; now you're tall. You used to be blonde and have blue eyes; now you're dark with brown eyes!"

The man, startled, said, "What are you, nuts or something? My name's not Walberg!"

"Oy, even your name you changed!"

Nat met a girl at a resort in Lakewood whom he found quite attractive. Unfortunately, the feeling was not mutual. He asked for her home number so he could get in touch with her in the City. She hesitated.

He decided on new tactics and began talking about his Rolls Royce, his penthouse apartment on the East Side, his prosperous business. Again, he asked for her 'phone number.

Once more, she hesitated. To avoid further embarrassment, she said, "I'll 'phone you. Where can you be reached?"

Elated, he said, "At the candy store on the corner! The number is SP 8-4692. Any evening at all...they'll call me!"

Two women sat on the porch of a hotel in Lakewood.

One said to the other, "Mine watch stopped going just before I came here so I took it back to Tiffany to be repaired. If you'll be so kindly, would you mind telling me what time it is on your watch?"

"Not at all! It's exactly five rubies after seven diamonds!"

In most synagogues, the regular parishioners are assigned seats for services held on the high Holy Days. To obtain additional revenue, seats are sold to others for these services as well. This is always done in advance of the holidays for many orthodox Jews do not carry money on the Holy Days. Also, it is a general practice to hire non-Jews as ticket takers.

In a small *shule** in the Bronx, on the Day of Atonement, a Jew tried to go in without a ticket. He was stopped at the door by the attendant. The Jew was adamant. He insisted that it was urgent that he go in to speak to his partner who was sitting in next to the last row. Again, he was refused admittance. He pleaded that it was a real emergency and that he'd be inside for only a few minutes.

The attendant finally relented but admonished him, "Remember...just for a couple of minutes and mind you...no praying!"

---

*Shule—*Yiddish for synagogue.*

The two senior partners in Pitzick and Pupkowitz, Inc. joined a country club and played golf on week-ends.

In the locker room one day, they overheard one of the members telling about the wonderful time he had had moose-hunting in the Maine woods.

The partners decided, as a change, they'd try moose-hunting on their vacations. And so they went down to Abercrombie and Fitch, out-fitted themselves, moose horns and all, and off they went to the Maine woods.

On their first day out, they hunted all day but all they got was mosquito-bitten. Pitzick wanted to quit but Pupkowitz said, "It won't get dark for an hour yet. Let's keep trying. Maybe our luck will change."

Nothing happened so they decided to head back to the lodge. They kept going around in circles and couldn't seem to find their way. To make matters worse, Pitzick fell into a deep hole. Pupkowitz tried to help his panicky partner but he fell into the hole instead.

They cried for help but no one heard them. It began to get dark and cold and they began to shake with fear. They took turns blowing on the moose horn. No one came to their rescue. They decided to yell, "Help! Help!" together until they were about to drop from exhaustion.

All of a sudden, they thought they heard from a distance, "Hello down there." The "hello down there" seemed to be getting closer and closer, until finally the voice seemed right above them.

Pitzick called up, "Who are you?"

"We're from the Red Cross," came the rejoinder.

"Oh," said Pupkowitz, "We gave already from the business!"

"Make up my bill 'cause I'm checking out!" said Mrs. Mandelbaum to the desk clerk at Rappaport's Rendez-vous in the Catskills.

"Is something wrong?" asked the clerk.

"Plenty is wrong! The food here...it's like poison! And such small portions yet!"

Two men were finishing their dinner in an East Side restaurant and were ready for the beverage.

The waiter asked, "A glass of tea maybe or maybe you want coffee?"

The first man said, "For a change, I think I'll have a glass of milk."

His friend followed with, "Make mine milk too but be sure the glass is clean!"

The waiter went back into the kitchen and brought out a tray with the two glasses of milk.

Addressing the men, he asked, "Which one of you gentlemen asked for the clean glass?"

Many years ago when the book, "The Well of Loneliness" was published, it caused quite a stir. Everyone was reading it.

A famous Hollywood producer called in one of his assistants and ordered him to buy the movie rights of the book.

His assistant protested. "You can't make a movie of that book! It's about lesbians!"

"So, we'll change it! We'll call them 'Austrians'!" persisted the producer.

Nouveau-riche Mrs. Birnbaum was planning a big party in her new home in Westchester. She had heard the "in" thing to do was to have music to entertain her guests. She 'phoned a talent agency and inquired about hiring a soprano for the evening.

"I would recommend Madame Romano."

"Is she good?" queried Mrs. Birnbaum.

"Good? Why, madam, she's a great virtuoso!"

"Never mind about her morals. What I'm interested in is: can she sing?"

Two-hundred and fifty pound Mrs. Shlump sat down at the breakfast table at Shimkin's Rendezvous-House in the Catskills. She greeted the ladies at her table and motioned to the waiter to take her order.

"First, I'll have a glass of hot water with lemon, then a large glass fig juice, then a plate of prunes, then a bowl of bran-flakes with a raw apple cut up in little pieces, coffee and bran muffins."

Turning to her table companions, she said reassuringly, "You see? Nothing for me; everything for the bowels!"

Golf had become an obsession with Minerva but, unfortunately, the only golf club near her home was a restricted one.

Her name sounded more German than Jewish and she wanted to see if she would be accepted. She passed.

Everything was fine until one day while playing with three of the other gals, she swung and missed! Without thinking, she yelled, "Oy! Gevalt!" and smiling sweetly, she added, "Whatever that means!"

A woman was walking in the street. She was startled to see her psychiatrist running down the street with a couch on his back.

She rushed up to him and said, "Dr. Shnure, what are you doing?"

"Making house calls!"

A "noodnick"* is a naked Santa Claus.

*Noodnick is Jewish for a pesty bore.

81

Upon graduating from high school, Young Martin went on to college and majored in botany. Poppa wanted him to study business administration and go into the millinery business as a junior partner. But Martin assured Poppa that if his career as a botanist did not work out well, he would then enter the business.

Martin became engrossed in his work and began to grow rare specimens of orchids. Poppa became interested in his son's hobby and from time to time, would sit down with him and ask him about his work.

In one of these heart-to-hearts, Martin told his father he had had a strange experience the day before. While sitting in a restaurant, a very attractive young lady came in and sat down opposite him. She began to talk to him and told him she was a stranger in town and very lonesome. Since he had no particular plans for the evening, he asked whether she'd like to come up to his apartment and see his collections of rare orchids. She said something like, "What! No etchings!" and they went up to the apartment.

He showed her the various specimens and she seemed completely disinterested and yawned continually.

"I finally suggested," said Martin, "That perhaps she'd like to come into the bedroom," and she quickly said, "Now you're talking!" and I continued, "To see my rare specimen of black orchid!"

Martin went on: "When we entered the bedroom, she began to take her dress off." I said to her, "You are obviously not interested in orchids!"

Poppa said, "That's what you said? But what did you do?"

"Nothing! But I came to a definite conclusion! You can lead a horse to water but you can't lead a horticulture."

Moishe was hired as a bus driver and given a route in East New York in a lonely, deserted neighborhood. He drove into the garage and sheepishly turned in the receipts of his first day's run, which amounted to $11.75.

The next day, he arrived bright and early, took out the bus but was not seen by any of the inspectors along his route. No one seemed to know what had happened to him or his bus.

At the end of the day, he turned up at the depot and with a grand flourish, turned in one hundred and twenty-eight dollars! The cashier was amazed and said, "What is this? No one ever turned in that much money for that run before. How did you do it?"

"You think I'm a fool?" beamed Moishe. "I said to myself why should I waste my valuable time on that God-forsaken route and drive practically an empty bus? So I turned in and drove along Pitkin Avenue and, believe me, it's a regular gold mine over there!"

Nathan got letter after letter from his family and friends who had gone to America to make their fortunes. He decided to go too. He had very little money but a great deal of pride and would not write for passage money. So he booked on a disreputable old ship. The trip would take a little longer but Nathan had plenty of time. After the ship was at sea for six days, a storm came up. The ship began to rock and pitch. Everyone on the boat was sick. Word began to spread that the ship was in danger of sinking. Pandemonium broke out. People everywhere were crying and praying!

Nathan stood around apparently unconcerned by what was going on.

One of the passengers noticed how calm he seemed and cried out:

"How can you be so composed and unconcerned when the ship is sinking?"

"Why should I worry?" answered Nathan. "Do I own the ship?"

A young Jewish soldier, going home on furlough, crawled into the upper berth of the train all set for a good night's sleep. Just as he was falling asleep, he heard a deep sigh coming from the lower berth and a woman's voice saying plaintively, "Oy! Am I thirsty!"

He turned over but each time he was about to lapse into unconsciousness, the same irritating "Oy! Am I thirsty!" woke him.

Annoyed to the point of bursting, he decided to get up and bring the pesty woman a glass of water so he could get some sleep.

He went to the end of the car, got a paper cup of water and handed it to the woman with a hasty "Here, here's some water."

He climbed back up to the upper berth.

Just as he was falling asleep, the quiet was shattered with a deep sigh and the same voice that boomed, "Oy! Was I thirsty!"

MOMMA
AND POPPA

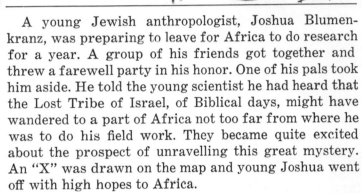

A young Jewish anthropologist, Joshua Blumenkranz, was preparing to leave for Africa to do research for a year. A group of his friends got together and threw a farewell party in his honor. One of his pals took him aside. He told the young scientist he had heard that the Lost Tribe of Israel, of Biblical days, might have wandered to a part of Africa not too far from where he was to do his field work. They became quite excited about the prospect of unravelling this great mystery. An "X" was drawn on the map and young Joshua went off with high hopes to Africa.

As soon as he could manage it, he travelled to the spot marked on the map. He found a thriving village but was surprised to find the people were black. He rationalized that with intermarriage through the thousands of years, this fact alone could not rule out the possibility that this was the Lost Tribe. They were practically naked except for bits of clothing, beads, war paint and feathers. He could accept this too. He approached various groups hoping to hear them speak Hebrew. Instead, he heard a strange mumbo-jumbo.

He realized he had come on a fool's errand. Discouraged, he was just about to leave when he noticed a man being carried on a stretcher from a tent. This would be the true test. The man was obviously dying or perhaps dead. If these people had retained the customs and language of their Hebrew fore-fathers, certainly a prayer for recovery or kaddish* for the dead would be chanted now.

As the body was placed on a stand a man, obviously a witch doctor, started to chant and throw what appeared to be holy water on the prostrate figure. Our anthropologist came nearer and again the chant turned out to be the same mumbo-jumbo he had heard previously. Disheartened, he started to leave when he noticed an elderly woman who seemed to be edging toward him. He waited. The old lady nudged him, pointed to the witch doctor, and said proudly, "Mine son-in-law, the doctor!"

---

*Kaddish—*Hebrew prayer for the departed.*

Two elderly women were talking while sunning themselves in the solarium of a Miami Beach hotel.

"Have I got a son!" boasted one of the women. "All my good friends should have a son like him! Did you see the mink stole I was wearing last night? He bought it for me. And you see this gorgeous diamond ring? My son bought it!"

The other woman, not to be outdone, said very proudly, "Mine dear, I have a wonderful son too! You shouldn't think you're the only one! My son is very successful too. He goes to the most expensive psychiatrist. Every afternoon he goes there, lays down on the couch and what do you think he talks about? Me!"

The sons of Solomon Berger noticed that their father had become argumentative. He had been a hard-working but rather mild man all his life. They thought this change might be a prelude to dotage and perhaps psychiatric help might forestall it. They arranged that he visit a psychiatrist.

For two weeks, four times a week, he entered the office, was shown to the couch and immediately fell sound asleep.

One of the sons contacted the psychiatrist to find out what sort of progress he was making. He was told his father fell into a deep sleep at each session and that nothing much had been accomplished. The doctor suggested that if the sons talked to him, he might make some effort to stay awake.

There was a family conference.

"Papa," one of the sons pleaded, "Please try to stay awake. It's costing us twenty-five dollars a visit!"

"Twenty-five dollars a visit?" queried papa, hardly believing his ears.

"Yes, papa. So please try to stay awake and talk to the doctor. Do your sleeping at home on your own time!"

Papa said he'd try.

The following morning, the old man was back at the psychiatrist's office and was shown to the couch. He kept his eyes wide open.

The doctor said, "Mr. Berger, before I ask you any questions, is there anything you'd like to ask me?"

"There sure is! Tell me doctor...maybe you need a partner?"

At a meeting in a large auditorium, someone cried out, "Is there a doctor in the house?"

An attractive young man jumped up and said, "I'm a doctor."

From the rear of the room, Mrs. Resnick jumped up and declared, "Oy! Have I got a daughter for you!"

85

Chicken soup, often referred to as "Jewish penicillin," was the panacea for all ills in most Jewish homes. It was administered to all the Irish and Italian neighbors as well. And it usually worked!

The Kaminskys were so poor that their home was practically threadbare. But mama and papa managed to scrape together enough money to buy two live chickens which they kept in the back yard. It was important that the children have fresh eggs.

But one of the chickens became sickly.

One night papa came home and noticed that there was only one chicken romping around in the yard.

"Where's the other chicken, mama?"

"I killed the healthy one to make chicken soup for the sickly one!"

Morris Rifkin complained that he was an absolute wreck, that for months he had not been able to sleep.

"The trouble with you," said his partner, "you don't relax. You take your troubles to bed with you!"

"You're absolutely right," answered Morris. "But what can I do? My wife refuses to sleep alone!"

Old man Willy Blumenfield was getting on in years. His son, Harold, had done well financially in ladies' underwear. He asked his father if he'd like to go down to Miami Beach. He thought it would be good for the old man to have companionship and balmy weather as well in his declining years.

The old man was pleased but consented to go only if he could be at a Kosher* hotel. And so Harold made reservations at the Sterling Hotel and put his father on a plane for Miami Beach.

His son 'phoned him once a week and everyone seemed happy. Some weeks later, Harold had to make a business trip south and decided to drop in on pop unannounced as a surprise.

When he got to the Sterling Hotel, there was no sign of old man Blumenfield. He asked the desk clerk if he had any idea where his father might be and he was told he might try room 402 at the Sans Souci. Harold was nonplussed but hopped into a cab and headed for the Sans Souci. He learned at the desk that room 402 was occupied by a Miss Peggy Murphy.

Harold rushed up to room 402, knocked at the door which was opened by a tall, sparsely dressed redhead.

And there was papa in a bathrobe!

Harold was furious! Unable to contain himself, he screamed, "Papa, I'm so shocked I don't know what to say! An old religious man like you! And you insisted yet you must stay at a kosher hotel!"

The old man looked at him as if crazy and said, "So, what are you getting so excited for? I dun't eat here!"

---

*Observing the orthodox Jewish dietary laws.

86

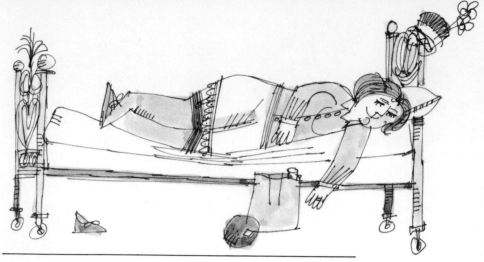

Moe Hirshorn's mother lived with him. She could easily have worn the crown of the Jewish Mrs. Malaprop.

One day after she had been shopping, she told her son, "I was so tired, I laid prostitute on the bed!"

The Lefkowitz boys decided to do something different for mama's birthday. Each year they had given her extravagant gifts like furs or jewelry or expensive perfume. But mama hardly ever went out and the gifts just decorated her apartment and closets instead of mama herself.

Since mama lived alone and probably needed company, her sons decided to give her a parrot for her birthday. Mama's English was what one would call "gahocked"* so they tried to find a parrot that spoke Yiddish.

They went from pet shop to pet shop and finally learned of an old man who had a bird that spoke Yiddish exclusively. They approached him but he refused to part with his pet. They kept raising the ante until he finally decided to sell his parrot with the assurance that it would get a good home. And he would also get seven hundred and fifty dollars.

They bought a shiny new cage, decorated it with pretty red bows and had it delivered by a singing Western Union boy who handed it to Mrs. Lefkowitz as he warbled "Happy birthday to you!"

The next day when the boys 'phoned mama, she thanked them. "Boyiss, you shouldna' done it. A birthday card would have been more than enough. And why did you have to go to the expense of paying a boychick to sing yet?"

"But, mama, you didn't say anything about the parrot. How was it?"

"Delicious!" answered mama, smacking her lips!

---

*Gahocked—*fractured in Yiddish.*

Mama Goldberg lived in a hotel for senior citizens in Long Beach. She was very happy there and her sons visited her regularly.

They had become successful in the business papa had left them and they showered mama with gifts to show their appreciation and love.

One Chanukah*, the boys came up with a great idea. They knew that mama no longer went visiting but stayed close to the hotel. She had all the jewelry and mink and frivolous things that she could ever use. Why not run her a party for her friends at the hotel?

They went to the 21 Club and ordered some magnums of champagne, a pound of the finest imported black caviar along with other delicacies.

Her sons drove out on the following Sunday and mama regaled them with stories of the beautiful party she had given, how they sang and danced the twist and had a wonderful time, thanks to the "boyiss." "Only one thing, my darlings, and you shouldn't be insulted if I tell you. I think maybe you should take next time from another delicatessen. The blackberry jam tasted from herring and the Dr. Brown's Celery Tonic was sour!"

Obviously upset, Mrs. Steingut paid a visit to a private detective agency.

She proceeded to tell the manager of her husband's extramarital affair with a certain blonde. In giving him the details, she painted a rather uncomplimentary picture of her spouse.

Finally, she said, "I want you should have one of your detectives follow my husband and this woman night and day. And then I want a complete report on what she sees in him."

Old man Berkowitz lay dying and asked that the rabbi be called. His grief-stricken wife and children huddled about the bed. The old man took his wife's hand and with eyes half-closed said faintly, "Is our eldest son, Louie, here?"

"Yes, papa, I'm here."

"And Avram, is he here?"

"Yes, papa, I'm here too."

"And Benny, is he by the bed too?"

"Yes, papa, I'm here."

"You're here too? So who's minding the store?"

---

*Chanukah—*Jewish Festival of Lights.*

Stanley Gilbert 'phoned the candy store on Rivington Street and asked, "Would you be good enough, please, to call my mother, Mrs. Goldberg, to the telephone?"

Mama came to the telephone and with a worried voice said, "Oy! Stanley, what happened? I know when I'm called to the telephone, it can't be good news!"

Stanley assured her that all was well. The decorator had finished furnishing his new apartment on Park Avenue. He was having a house-warming on the following Sunday from three to seven. Naturally, he told her, he wanted her to come. She promised she would and he asked that she come early, even before three.

The party was in full swing on Sunday and there was no sign of mama. Stanley became worried and 'phoned the candy store to find out if mama maybe got sick. The candy store owner rang her bell and said no one answered.

At seven, the guests started leaving and still there was no sign of mama. After all the guests had departed, he thought he had better hop in a cab and rush down to his mother's house. He 'phoned down to the doorman to hail a cab.

When he got down to the lobby, there was mama sitting on a bench, all dressed up, hands folded in her lap.

"Mama," he shrieked, "Are you all right? Why didn't you come upstairs?"

Of course, I'm all right," calmly answered mama. "Only I forgot your name!"

A wealthy underwear manufacturer named Aaron Dubinsky had a severe stroke and thought his end was in sight. He motioned for his wife, Bella, to come to his bedside. He had something to tell her. He had always planned on making a will but never got to it.

"So listen to what I tell you, Bella. I want to leave the business to Stanley."

"Why to Stanley?" implored his wife. "You know he'll take the whole profits and run to the track and before you know it, there'll be no business. Better you should leave it to Montgomery."

"All right, so I'll leave it to Montgomery. The car, I want should go to Daniel."

"Why to Daniel? He lives in the city. He don't need a car. Better you should leave it to Rosalie. She could use it where she lives in Long Island."

"Rosalie then gets the car. Our summer home in Liberty, I want to leave to our daughter, Deborah."

"Deborah's husband is a rich advertising executive. If she wants a summer home, let him buy it for her. Better you should leave it to Sylvia...her husband don't do so well financially."

"Look, Bella," said Aaron weakly, "Who's dying around here...you or me?"

Papa was eighty-two and began to act a bit childish. His children were naturally concerned. They decided to call in a psychiatrist.

A Dr. Cooper came and asked papa to lie down on the couch and to keep his eyes closed. He asked the old man question after question. He asked him to raise one arm, put it down, raise one leg, put it down and so on ad infinitum. This went on for about an hour and papa did everything requested of him. Then he nodded his head, pretended he had fallen asleep.

Finally, the psychiatrist left saying that he would submit his report after further study.

Papa opened one eye and said to his son, "Tell me, Simon, the 'meshuggeneh',* did he leave already?"

*Meshuggeneh—*Yiddish for "crazy one"*.

LOVE,
MARRIAGE,
AND SEX

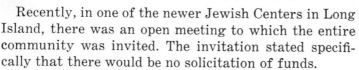

Recently, in one of the newer Jewish Centers in Long Island, there was an open meeting to which the entire community was invited. The invitation stated specifically that there would be no solicitation of funds.

After a short business meeting, the speaker of the evening was introduced.

He started his speech by saying: "Ladies and gentlemen. Before I go into my prepared text, I'd like to deliver a few remarks on sex appeal."

A little old Jewish lady in the last row nudged her friend and said, "Oy! Beckie, I'm dying!...Another appeal!"

Molly gave birth to triplets. As soon as she heard the good news, her friend, Bessie, came to see her bringing her home-made chicken soup and "God forbid you should need it," stewed prunes.

"Molly dear, I just can't believe you actually had triplets! Oy, it's marvelous!"

"Marvelous?" said Molly. "Why the doctor told me it's practically a miracle! He told me triplets happen only once in one million, six hundred and eighty times!"

"Oh, my God, Molly, when did you have time to do your housework?"

Hymie Rottenberg put a dime in the 'phone slot and dialed a number. A female voice answered, "Cunningham and Benton."

He said, "I'd like to speak to Mr. Sexauer, please."

The voice said, "Mr. who?"

Mr. Rottenberg repeated, "Mr. Sexauer, please!"

Again, she said, "Who?"

Annoyed, Hymie said, "Miss, don't you have a Sexauer there?"

"Mister, we don't even have a coffee break!"

The program chairman of the men's club of a Jewish Center decided to do something different by way of a program to entertain the members. He arranged to have a psychologist address the next meeting on the subject of sex. He advised the speaker that the meeting would start promptly at 8:30 and the speaker was on time. He was shown to a seat on the platform.

The president called the meeting to order. The invocation was read, followed by the reading of lengthy minutes. Next came a procession of chairmen of various committees who apparently were infatuated with the sound of their voices. Then came a discussion of old business and new.

The members were fidgeting in their seats impatient to hear the guest speaker for the hour was getting late. Finally, the president said, "And now it gives me great pleasure to introduce the speaker of the evening," and he droned on and on in his lengthy introduction while the members fidgeted some more with many eyes glancing towards the clock on the wall.

Finally, the president said, "And so without further ado, it gives me great pleasure to introduce to you Dr. Jonas whose subject will deal with sex."

The speaker arose.

He said, "Ladies and gentlemen. It gives me great pleasure!" And he sat down.

What's the difference between a French woman, an English woman and a Jewish woman being kissed in bed by her husband?

The French woman says, "Oo, Gaston! Your kisses! Oo la la!"

The English woman says, "'By Jove, Clive! You kiss jolly well!"

The Jewish woman says, "You know, Jake,...the ceiling needs a painting!"

A little old Jewish lady rushed up to a policeman and cried out, "Oy! Officer, officer...I've been raped!"

Startled, the policeman quickly took out his notebook and pen and said, "You have, madam? When?"

"Twenty-two years ago!"

Annoyed, the policeman said, "Twenty-two years ago! Well, why are you telling it to me now?"

Lowering her gaze, she sheepishly answered, "'Cause I like to talk about it."

Louie Abrams came home from the shop earlier than usual and found his wife in the arms of a stranger.

He went over to the table, banged on it and bellowed: "Company or no company...I want mine supper!"

Dejectedly, Morris Friedman entered the doctor's examination room. The doctor asked what his complaint was.

"Doctor, I don't know what's wrong with me. The first time I make love to mine wife, I feel good. I'm warm, I'm comfortable and I feel good. The next time, I'm cold, I'm shivering, mine teeth are chattering. There must be something wrong with me!"

The doctor said he had never had anyone come to him with that kind of a problem but he would give him a complete physical. He was given all sorts of tests and the doctor could find nothing wrong with him. He suggested he send his wife to him for a consultation.

Mrs. Friedman arrived.

"Your husband has come to me with a very strange complaint. I've given him a very thorough examination and I find nothing particularly wrong with him physically. Perhaps, you can fill in some of the gaps. He tells me that the first time he makes love to you, he's warm and comfortable and the next time, he's so cold that he actually shivers."

She looked at him, nodding her head scornfully.

"You call yourself a doctor? For this your father had to slave to send you to medical school? The first time is July; the next time, it's December!"

The young man was reproaching the marriage broker.

"You call yourself an honest 'shadchen'.* I put my faith in you and you lied to me about the girl you introduced me to!"

"Why, wasn't she a beautiful girl, like I told you?"

"Yes, she was a good-looking girl."

"Wasn't she smart like I told you?"

"She was smart enough."

"Didn't I tell you she plays the piano like a doll?"

"Yes, she plays the piano all right. But you told me she comes from a fine family with a good background and that her father was dead. She herself told me her father has been in jail for the past eight years!"

"Nu... I ask you? Do you call that living?" asked the shadchen.

A Jewish Texan, Rhett Skulnick, checked into the Waldorf with his wife. They were about to step out for the evening, when she discovered that she had forgotten to bring along a girdle.

She asked her husband to please go down to the specialty shop in the lobby and buy her a girdle size 27.

Sheepishly, he walked in and an attractive young lady asked if she could be of assistance to him.

"I'd like a girdle in size 27."

The sales girl inquired, "Do you wanna Playtex?"

"Ah sure do, sweetie, but ah can't make it tonight. I'll call you first thing tomorra!"

---

*Shadchen—Yiddish for marriage-broker.

Len Adler was cruising along in his white convertible. He noticed an attractive young lady walking along the avenue. He honked his horn, ogled her and she entered the car.

After an evening on the town, they sat in the car petting. He suggested that they go up to his apartment but she seemed unwilling. He tried persuasion, describing his beautiful penthouse with a view. Perhaps, they could have a drink, dance and spend the night there. She resisted.

"But why?" he implored.

"Why, I'd hate myself in the morning!"

"I have a solution," coaxed Lou. "Sleep late!"

Private first-class Herschel Blumenschmeir was sent overseas and was gone for sixteen months. When he returned, he found his wife, Gittel, with a new baby four months old.

He was greatly disturbed.

He began to question her, "Was it Elliott Lefkow?"

"No!"

"Was it Wally Salzman?"

"No!"

"Was it Pincus Reinhart?"

"No!"

Outraged, he walked over to his faithless wife, smacked her across the face and bellowed, "What's the matter? My friends ain't good enough for you?"

Montague Rhinestone, wholesale furrier and bon vivant, hired a new model for his showroom.

She was gorgeous, red-headed, willowy and willing... to go out with the boss.

On their first date, they dined and danced and wound up in his apartment. After a few drinks with the hi-fi playing Jackie Gleason's music for lovers, he put his arm around her and kissed her. All of a sudden, he started blowing vigorously into her beautifully coiffured hair.

Annoyed because he was ruining her hair-do, she whined, "What are you doing that for?"

"Gee, kiddo, I guess I got carried away! Once a furrier, always a furrier!"

A little elderly Jewish painter was hired to paint the inside of the house. He painted the bedroom first. That night, the owner, Dr. Roth, inspected the paint job. He put his hand on the wall saying that it looked pretty dry. His hand left an imprint and he was distressed about having marked the newly painted wall. His wife, Jennie, assured him the painter could touch it up.

The next morning, the old man arrived and began mixing his paints to start work on the kitchen.

Mrs. Roth said to the painter, "Before you start on the kitchen, come into the bedroom. I want to show you where my husband put his hand last night."

"Please, missus," said the painter, "I'm already an old man. If you do wanna do me a favor, give me better a glass of tea with lemon!"

Seventy year old Morris began complaining about aches and pains. After much nagging on the part of Rifka, he made an appointment with Dr. Starrsky.

When he came home, Rifka said, "Nu, so what did the doctor say?"

"Well, for a man my age, he said I'm pretty healthy. The only thing wrong is I got a little heart condition."

Alarmed, Rifka wailed, "Oy, gevalt*...so what'll be?"

"So nothing will be! He said I'll be all right, only I gotta cut down on everything a little...on eating, on working, on everything. Even on love-making, he said I got to cut down. He said for a man my age, semi-annually is enough. By the way, Rifka, how many times a month is 'semi-annually'?"

Everyone is familiar with the statement, "Any reference to persons living or dead is co-incidental." That does not apply here for the following is a true story. Since one of the characters involved is still alive, their names will be omitted:

A famous Jewish playwright lived with an actress of a different faith for many years in one of the capitals of Europe. Among his friends were the so-called intelligentsia...artists, writers, politicos...all Jewish.

One day, his friends were startled to receive invitations to the wedding of their famous playwright friend and his actress lady-love. They went to the wedding, of course, but not before they sent a telegram to the groom which read, "Ma nishtana halileh hazay mikoll hollalose?"*

---

*Gevalt—*help in Yiddish.*
*A passage contained in the Passover service which translated, is *"Whyfore is this night different from all other nights?"*